THE LAST
OF THE
SHOR
SHAMANS

First published by Moon Books, 2008
Moon Books is an imprint of John Hunt Publishing Ltd., Laurel House, Station Approach,
Alresford, Hants, SO24 9JH, UK
office1@jhpbooks.net
www.johnhuntpublishing.com
www.moon-books.net

For distributor details and how to order please visit the 'Ordering' section on our website.

Text copyright: A & L Arbachakov 2008

ISBN: 978 1 84694 127 6

A CIP catalogue record for this book is available from the British Library.

Design: Stuart Davies

Cover Photo of Vasilii Savel'evich Ady'yakov, by Alexander Arbachakov

Printed and bound by CPI Group (UK) Ltd, Croydon, CR0 4YY

We operate a distinctive and ethical publishing philosophy in all
areas of our business, from our global network of authors to
production and worldwide distribution.

THE LAST
OF THE
SHOR
SHAMANS

Alexander & Luba Arbachakov

Winchester, UK
Washington, USA

CONTENTS

ENDORSEMENTS

"The publication of Alexander and Luba Arbachakov's 2004 study of Shamanism in their own community in Siberia is an important addition to the study of the anthropology and sociology of the peoples of Russia. Joanna Dobson's excellent English translation of the Arbachakov's work brings to a wider international audience a fascinating glimpse into the rapidly disappearing traditional world of the Shor Mountain people. That the few and very elderly Shortsi Shamans were willing to share their beliefs and experiences with the Arbachakov's has enabled us all to peer into this mysterious and mystic world."
Frederick Lundahl, Retired American Diplomat and Specialist on Central Asia and former Soviet Union countries.

"This book is a most worthy contribution to our knowledge of Siberian shamanism, illuminating the shamanic traditions of the little-known Shor ethnic group. The documentation is all the more valuable since the research has been done and recorded by native Shor ethnographers so that the observations and language of the shamanic rituals are, without question, authentic and represent a true picture of historical traditions and current cultural adaptations. Particularly important for preservation are the interviews with, and observations of, Shor shamans who were practicing in the post-Soviet period, and the documentation and translation of their kamlanie chants."
Eva Jane Neumann Fridman, Ph.D., author of *Sacred Geography: Shamanism Among the Buddhist Peoples of Russia* and co-author of *Shamanism: An Encyclopedia of World Beliefs, Practices, and Culture.*

"I welcome the publication of this volume by Shor ethnographers on Shor shamans. Their insider insights are enhanced with shamanic texts and ritual descriptions collected in the nick of time, as knowledgeable elderly Siberian shamans of the magnificent Altai-Sayan mountains have been passing away".

Marjorie Mandelstam Balzer, Ph.D., Research Professor, Georgetown University, editor of the journal Anthropology and Archeology of Eurasia and the book *Shamanic Worlds*.

The Last of the Shor Shamans was originally published in Russian in 2004 under the sponsorship of Dream Change, Inc. as - *The Shamans of Gornaya Shoriya* - by the publishing house Kuznetskaya Krepost.

Translation of Russian text into English was completed in 2007 by Joanna Dobson, sponsored by Dream Change, Inc. and the Wilderness Wisdom Fund. This included direct translation of Shor shamanic verses by Altai scholar and historian, Brontoi Bedurev, and Altai elder and Kaichi (throat singer and keeper of the oral history and culture), Nogon Shumarev.

This book is dedicated to the Shortsi – children, students and adults alike - as they strive to rejuvenate the traditional culture of their ancient and unique people.

INTRODUCTION

In November of 1999 I embarked with Bill Pfeiffer, founder of the Sacred Earth Network (SEN), on an exploratory expedition to meet with Siberian shamans. The trip was a joint venture between the non-profit organizations SEN and Dream Change, Inc. (DC) - preparation for subsequent journeys that Bill and I would facilitate for North Americans and Europeans wishing to learn from traditional Siberian elders, ultimately in the Tuva and the Altai regions. Bill had journeyed for more than a decade to Russia with SEN to empower liaisons between U.S. and Siberian environmentalists. I had worked for many years through DC with indigenous shamanic peoples in Guatemala, the Andes of Ecuador, as well as with remote tribes in the Amazon Basin, facilitating expeditions that helped to preserve indigenous cultures and ancestral lands, and that encouraged the application of traditional wisdom approaches to modern social and environmental problems.

Our first destination on this joint trip to southern Siberia was to visit the indigenous peoples living in Shor territory within the Shor Mountain region. Bill and I were fortunate to have two indigenous guides and the authors of this book, Alexander and Luba Arbachakov, accompany us throughout our two-week trip. The Shor people number just over 10,000 and during the 20th century have been decimated by repression, alcohol and suicide. Still, they have managed to save their language and a few remnants of their culture. During the time of our stay many of the Shor shamans were in their 70's and 80's and not easy subjects for westerners to visit without inside connection with trusted Shor members. The grandparents of many of these shamans were the renowned Siberian 'drumming' shamans, persecuted during the Soviet occupation from the 1920's to 1980's - arrested, jailed, forced to give up their beliefs and practices, even shot in the back or rounded up and burned alive. As a result, these - now older - Shor shamans were few in number, protective about their 'shamanizing' (conducting shamanic rituals), and rarely experienced outside of their isolated indigenous boundaries. Bill and I were the first outsiders these elders had experienced.

Thanks to the Arbachakovs, I am blessed to have met many Shortsi (as they are known), to have seen the exquisite beauty of their lands, rivers and mountains under the early winter snows, to have stayed in their humble wooden homes, enjoyed their saunas, witnessed the seasonal slaughter of animals in preparation for the long winter months, eaten foraged mushrooms, berries, and pine nuts from their root cellars, and most memorably, experienced ceremony from two of the shamanic peoples that Alexander and Luba Arbachakov present in this book.

During our time in Shor territory, Bill Pfeiffer and I sat in the kitchen of shaman Kirill Propkop'evich Chudekov who eyed us carefully as he ate from a bowl of raw garlic cloves. I'd become feverishly ill during the long, cold train journeys and, after determining our sincerity in seeking ceremony for me, Kirill agreed to perform kamlanie (shamanic ritual). His chanting was haunting and emotional. I felt as if ancient, ancestral spirits and those of the Shor lands were singing through him, piercing our ordinary reality with mysterious and hidden wisdom. Tears filled my eyes as I watched Kirill wave the worn dish towel he held in his hand as he chanted, his other hand meeting the towel with strong, brisk strokes as if beating an invisible drum. Religious oppression had broken the Shor tradition of passing and enlivening the drum and those shamanizing covertly during the Soviet period used dish towels or brooms in lieu of drums.

Several days later we met up with Evdokiya Gavrilovna Todyyakova whom we had tracked down a village away, because her house was unfit to live in during the cold months. During this time, she lived wherever she was welcomed often wandering from home to home. It was a cold, snowy night and the sharp smell of vodka saturated the car as she entered it. Evdokiya, who sat on my lap in the car, sang and laughed and I thought she was totally inebriated. Arriving at the home of our host after midnight, Evdokiya was given a cup of tea and told of our sincere interest in her shamanizing. We asked if she would do kamlanie for us. She looked at me intently without a trace of intoxication detectable; then said she'd do a pulse reading and simple cleansing. Evdokiya's shamanizing was focused and effective despite the late hour, her chanting as piercing as Kirill's.

Very little was known to the international public audience on the ancient history and spirituality of Siberia until the collapse of the Soviet Union in 1991. Many shamans braved death by practicing and teaching in secret during the years of repression throughout the Soviet reign. Prior to Perestroika, and as early as the 1700's, shamanic peoples were persecuted by Russian Orthodox Christian missionaries who viewed indigenous ways as backward. Although shamanism has again become a vital part of the lives of many Siberians such as with the Tuvan people as well as the Buryat peoples near Lake Baikal – many ancient indigenous languages are endangered and shamanism as an oral and living tradition is dying, or has died out, within Siberia groups such as the Ob-Ugric, the Nganansan and the Shor. The Shor shamanic legacy might not be remembered if not for a book such as this.

Evdokiya Gavrilovna Todyyakova

Photo: Llyn Roberts

Indigenous Shor themselves, Luba Arbachakov is a folklorist and expert on indigenous culture and spirituality, and Alexander Arbachkov is a photographer and was director for many years of his own NGO, the Agency for the Protection of the Taiga. In this beautiful compilation, Alexander and Luba bring together previously disparate information on Shor shamanism. From the first-hand perspective of their own fieldwork, they portray the world view, culture and rituals of the Shor and provide ethnographic sketches of some of the few remaining and contemporary shamans. Text of the shamanic verses of two of these Shor elders, previously unpublished in English, are presented here for the first time.

The Last of the Shor Shamans preserves the legacy of the shamans of the Shor Mountain region of Siberia and it may be the only way these shamans are remembered. Those who read with an engaged heart will open to the ancestors, spirits and living wisdom of the Shor mystical tradition.

Llyn Roberts, M.A.

Llyn Roberts is the author of *The Good Remembering, Shamanic Reiki*, and *Shapeshifting into Higher Consciousness* (all O-Books). Llyn directs the non-profit organization, Dream Change (founded by John Perkins - dedicated to applying indigenous wisdom for global and personal change), and conducts workshops in Europe and the U.S. at leading educational institutions such as the Omega Institute, Esalen, and Rowe Conference Center. Llyn lives and writes in Western Massachusetts and Whidbey Island, WA.

AUTHORS' FOREWORD

Studies into the culture and worldview of the Shor Siberian people were first conducted in the early eighteenth century. At that time, the Shortsi, Altai and Khakas peoples were still officially considered one ethnic group. As a result, for many years the spiritual culture of the Shortsi was not studied independently. It was only in the second half of the nineteenth century that researchers gradually began to concentrate on the Shortsi as an independent, unique cultural group.

The term 'Shortsi' was first introduced by the well known researcher and Turkologist V.V. Radlov at the end of the nineteenth century. He borrowed the term from one of the more numerous clans (sook – literally meaning 'bone') of the people – the 'Shortsi', who lived (and still live to this day) in the area of the upper reaches of the Kondom river. Radlov included all the native population settled in the Kondom and Mrassu river basins and the very upper reaches of the Tom under this one term. Developing this idea from the missionary priest and academic researcher B.I. Verbitski, he was the first to separate the Shortsi from their neighbouring peoples; close relatives both in terms of language and culture such as the Teleut, Kumandintsi, Chelkantsi, Altaitsi, and Abakanski Tatars (Khakas): " I have united the Tatars living on the Tom, Mrass and Kondom under the common term 'Shortsi'...I was prompted to this decision by the fact that they practically speak the same language which I refer to as the Shor dialect and the fact that the Teleuts and their western neighbours the Lebedintsi and Black Tatars refer to them all as 'Shor-kijhi', 'Shor people'. (Radlov, 1989, 209).

Participants of the second and third Russian academic expeditions in the eighteenth century headed by academics G.F. Miller and P.C. Pallas were the first to describe the way of life, culture and traditions of the Shortsi. In his book "Travels in Siberia" I.G. Gmelin, participant of the second expedition in 1734 records his meeting with a Shor shaman and describes the shaman's attributes: "...We called for a kam (Shor word for shaman) who was going to perform a ritual. He brought a drum with him which looked something like a sieve with one side covered in leather. On the hollow side a wooden rod was attached than ran vertically through the centre. In the middle where the kam held the drum the rod was thinner, moving into two goblet shapes, supposedly to intensify the sound, one either side of the hand and then tapering out again at the edges where the cross piece meets the frame. Both ends were triple-sided. Perpendicular to the wooden handle an iron rod is fixed on each side of which hang five hollow iron flinders. This rod runs horizontally, not through the middle but off centre and therefore is not held in the hand. The rattle is a flinder, removed and re-sewn in hare skin and decorated in ribbons and strings. The kam showed us the drum and rattle. At times he spoke in his own language and at others he bellowed like a bear. He would move back and forth or sit, pull terrible grimaces or making strange, frightening body movements his eyes either staring or closed like a mad-man." (Gmelin, 1994, 13-14).

Approximately one hundred years later the study of the history and ethnography of the Shortsi was continued by other prominent ethnographers such as V.V. Radlov, V.I. Verbitski, A.B. Adrianov and A.V. Anokhin.

V.V. Radlov and V.I. Verbitski (Radlov, 1989; Verbitski, 1893) were the first to describe the basis of the Shor spiritual worldview.

In his collected articles *Altaiskie Inorodtsi* Verbitski describes what he calls their 'faith' in the following manner: Essentially the Altai faith is based on the idea that two quintessential principles rule the world. These are benevolent Ul'gen and evil Erlik. To both, a great number of spirits are assigned. Light spirits 'arig neme' are assigned to Ul'gen and dark spirits 'kara neme' to Erlik...The mediator between the gods and man, the conductor of sacrificial ritual, diviner, sorcerer and likewise enemy is the 'kam' or shaman." (Verbitski, 1893, 61, 63).

In 1916 Anokhin conducted research into both Altai and Shor shamanic drums, studying ten Shor, eleven Kumandintsi, four Chelkantsi and three Black Tatar drums. During the process he also made a record of the genealogy of the shamans from the Shor clan 'kobi'. In the publication 'Kuznetskie Inorodtsi Tomskoi Guberni' Anokhin writes: 'The Shor shamanists acknowledge two different principles: benevolent Ul'gen and evil Erlik. Aside from Ul'gen and Erlyk the Shortsi also acknowledge the mountain spirits.' A.V. Anokhin described both the funeral rites and objects of the shamanic cult as separate themes in his work 'The shamanist funeral and characteristics of the shaman's vestments and idols etc'. Here he writes: 'Shamans are buried in the same manner as an ordinary deceased but more hurriedly. The drum and rattle of the deceased shaman, male or female, are hung to a tree in proximity to the grave. Close relatives remove a part from the drum, usually a metal flinder, chain or button which is kept as a relic. When a new young shaman relative appears then these relics are attached to their drum.' (Anokhin, 1918: ??, 1994, 62-63).

Later in the Soviet period the Shor belief system was also studied by N.P. Dyrenko, L.P. Potapov, N.A. Baskakov, I.D. Khlopina, G.F. Babushkin, N.A. Alekseev, A.I. Chudoyakov and V.M. Kimeev.

In her collected articles 'Shorski Folklop' N.P. Dyrenkova published the myths of Shor folklore concerning the deities, spirits and shamans. A significant portion of the unique material gathered by Dyrenkova on Shor shamanism was not actually included in her publication and is preserved in archives. This material mainly concerns information on spirit helpers, types of shamanic ritual - 'kamlanie' - and shamanic attributes used in ritual.

Complex research into the shamanism of Gornaya Shoriya was last carried out in 1977. At that time the ethnographic section of the Institute of Languages, Literature and History, Siberian Branch, Russian Academy of Science, USSR, collected data for a special, unified project on the religious conceptions and ceremonies of the Siberian Turkic peoples. The results of this work are reflected in academic N.A.Alekseev's monograph entitled 'Shamanism among the Turkic speaking peoples of Siberia', published in 1984.

Unfortunately, beginning with the colonization of the Shortsi in the seventeenth century and up until the end of the twentieth century, shamans and their followers have been endlessly persecuted. This initially began with missionaries who came to Siberia with the Russian pioneers. Clearly enjoying the support of the state, missionaries were successful in their attempts to convert the native population. Shamanism was considered a dark cult and shamans, servants of the devil. Missionary activities reached their peak in the nineteenth century when the Altai Spiritual Mission (Russian Christian organization created in the 1830's) consolidated its strength in Altai and Gornaya Shoriya. This resulted in the merciless persecution of both specific individuals and shamanism in general.

In the Soviet period shamans were categorised as enemies of the state and so sent to camps or simply shot. Drums and ritual clothing were burned and the graves of shamans desecrated. Soviet ideology trampled over the souls of the indigenous people like a heavy roller. Now, as a result of all these events, one only very rarely meets with an individual in a remote village - 'ulus' or 'aal' - who has managed to preserve the remains of ancient knowledge and knows how to heal the so-called 'shaman's illness'. Occasionally, for a purely symbolic sum these shamans will perform the mystery of communication with the spirits to help their fellow men.

Today, two types of shaman exist. There are those who continue the people's traditions of centuries and there are those new performing shamans who simply amuse the public with exotic show.

In this book we are concerned with the first type of shaman, the genuine shaman. These individuals represent the true guardians of their people's traditions, customs and culture. Sadly, with every passing year their number decreases. The most elderly pass away whilst the younger generation aspires to a different set of ideals, idols, culture and subculture. Civilization is now with us it seems.

This book focuses on Shor shamanism and on the last 'kam' shamans of Gornaya Shoriya, with whom we were able to meet and converse. Our work includes the main elements of Shor worldview and relationship to the forces and spirits believed to exist in Nature; a description of the processes of shamanic ritual - 'kamlanie' - and the never before printed texts of two shamanic verse.

It is our hope that this book will serve to create better understanding of the culture, history and traditions of the Shor Siberian people.

Alexander and Luba Arbachakov

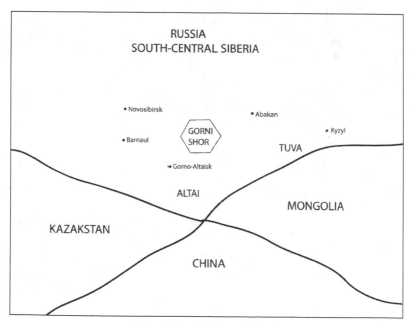

Map of Shor Territory, Siberia
Courtesy of the Sacred Earth Network

SHOR WORLD VIEW

The perception that the universe exists in three levels is typical of all the Turkic speaking peoples of Siberia. The Universe is said to be comprised of the Upper World, the Middle World and the Lower World or: 1) the World of the Heavens, 2) the Earth, and the 3) Under World - all of which are populated by human beings, animals, other living creatures and likewise by various deities and spirits.

The three worlds are connected via the axis of the World Tree or Mountain. The World Tree has its crown in the sky (the Upper World) whilst its trunk passes through the Middle World and its roots reach down into the ground (the Lower World). Similarly, **Shaman's Symbols**
the peak of the mountain is

Artist: Luba Arbachakov

connected to the sky and the foot of the mountain, to the Earth. This notion of the construction of the World is widespread among the many peoples of the Altai-Sayan region. It is illustrated on shamanic drums and is reflected in rituals and ceremonies in which the kam (shaman) journeys from the Earth's surface, the Middle World, either up into the sky or down into the earth.

The world tree is usually associated with the cedar (larch) or birch tree. As a rule shamanic rituals were carried out under birch trees and as such this tree was particularly revered. Aside from shamanic activities, the birch played an important role in a variety of different ceremonies including weddings.

The perception of the mountain as axis of the world was

projected onto one specific mountain that stood out from the others within a given territory either for its height or other peculiar characteristic. It was believed that the shaman's guardian spirit dwelt on this special mountain and that his life and fate were generally linked with it.

It is the function and calling of the kam (shaman) to act as mediator between the deities, spirits and humankind, and between the three worlds.

In his diaries of the 1927 Gornaya Shoriya expedition, Ethnographer I.D. Khlopina gives a description of the structure of the world based on conversations held with Shor shamans (Aleksei (ulus Ulabish), Tatyana and Nikolai (ulus Kechin), Darya (ulus Pizas)).

1. The Middle Earth - 'Ortinda Cheri' or 'Pistin Cher' – Our Earth.
2. The Under World - 'Aina Cheri' – land of evil spirits.
3. The Heavenly Realm. 'Ulgen Cheri'- Realm of Ulgen, the Sky.

1. The Middle Earth is flat and the Pistag/Mustag Mountain stands at its centre. During a 'kamlanie' (ceremonial ritual) addressed to Ul'gen, the 'che ezi' (master spirit of a given place) of the Pistag Mountain plays the most significant role among all other mountain spirits and spirit helpers.

Pistag (pis/mis – ice) is the centre, the navel of the Earth – 'cherdin kingigi'. At the foot of the mountain lies a lake in which the strong, old fish 'Ker palyk' abides. They say that when 'Ker palyk' moves, the Earth trembles.

2. The Underworld- is the realm of Erlik and his helpers, the evil spirits 'aina' who are capable of stealing a person's spirit – 'kut'. When a kam (shaman) conducts a healing ceremony for the sick he descends into the lower world, the realm of Erlik.

3. In the realm of Ul'gen there are nine skies. The first, yellow sky, is the realm of lightning which is said to be the whip of Ulgen's white horse – 'ak pozat'. When thunder is heard they say: 'Tegri

Shor Lands Under November Snow

kugrepcha, kudai kugrepcha ili Ul'gen kugrepcha' – 'the sky
thunders, God roars or Ul'gen roars'. The first layer of sky is
called 'keshkan'. The che ezi (master spirit) of this level, 'Samchi',
lives with his wife and children in the middle of the sky in a
dwelling the same as man's.

The second sky is called 'kok kur' – 'blue belt'. This is the
realm of the blue part of the rainbow – 'tegri chelize'. The red part
of the rainbow is present in the third part of the sky – 'kizil kur'.
The grey part of the rainbow is present in the fourth sky – 'kir
kur'. The blue part of the rainbow is present in the fifth sky
'kektamosh-kur'. The sixth sky is referred to as 'sky' rather than
'belt' and is called 'kizil tegri' – 'red sky'. It is here in the red sky
that the red women are said to live but of them nothing more is
known. The seventh sky is the realm of the moon and stars. The
eighth sky is the realm of the sun.

Ul'gen abides in the ninth sky where he has been known to
place rings around the sun and moon. In the ninth sky it is always
light and warm. The grass never dries out and the flowers never
fade. There is always an abundance of cattle and animals. Of the
ninth sky it is said: 'Osken odu kurulbas' – 'Where the grass

never withers', and 'Olgen kijhi chizelbes', 'where the body of the deceased never decays'.

When Ul'gen is addressed during a 'kamlanie' (shamanic ritual) he is requested to grant well-being, prosperity and fertility. 'Ul'gen may grant a man anything'. (Khlopina, 1992, p. 135-6).

A Shor creation myth reads in the following manner:

In the beginning, when there was nothing in the world but emptiness, the higher deity 'Kudai-Ul'gen' became bored and so in the emptiness he created three skies. In the lower sky he placed his son Paktan – Pugra. In the middle sky he placed the spirit Keikush and in the upper sky he lived with his wife Chaashin (according to another version she is 'Solton'). In order to fill the remaining emptiness Ul'gen also created the Sun, moon and stars and then the smooth, even earth and her rivers.

U'lgen's younger brother Erlik observing his brother decided that he too should take part in the creation process and so he fixed the mountains on the Earth. The most beautiful of these was 'Sogra' mountain. Erlik rose to the top of the mountain and there created the birds and animals.

Whilst Erlik was busy creating the mountains and the animals Ul'gen set about creating man and as he did not know how to create man's soul he set out in search of it. He made dog guard man in his absence. Erlik had been watching Ul'gen and as soon as he left Erlik walked up to man; created, but soulless. Dog growled and refused to let him pass. Seeing that dog had no fur Erlik said: "You will be cold in winter with no fur. Let me approach man and I shall give your body fur." Dog agreed and let Erlik pass. Immediately his body was covered in fur. Erlik walked freely up to man, spat on him, rubbed dirt on him and then left.

A little later not having found man's soul Ul'gen returned and saw that man was rubbed in dirt and that dog was covered in fur. He interrogated dog who told him everything. Ul'gen thought about Erlik and began to suspect that Erlik knew how to create man's soul. He called Erlik and asked him directly. Erlik replied that he did indeed know how to create man's soul but added that if he made man's soul it would belong entirely to him and only the body would belong to Ul'gen. Left with no other option Ul'gen was forced to accept. Erlik went into the taiga (Siberian evergreen forest) and picked a hollow angelica stem, a 'kobrak' from which he made a tube. He walked up to man and placed the tube into his mouth. Then, he blew man's soul threw the tube and into his body. When a person dies they say that Erlik takes the soul back, which after death is referred to as 'uzut'.

Ul'gen became angry at Erlik and decided to ban him from the Earth leaving him with nowhere to live. Hearing of Ul'gen's decision Erlik came to him in despair. He wept and complained that he had nowhere to live and pleaded with Ul'gen to relinquish him some small corner of land but Ul'gen remained implacable. Then Erlik asked for the mere spot on the ground where the end of Ul'gen's staff rested. Ul'gen agreed but as soon as he raised his staff from the ground all kinds of vermin, snakes and insects began to crawl out of the hole onto the Earth's surface. Erlik climbed down into the hole where he lives to this day, under the ground.

Ul'gen was horrified by the terrible quantity of vermin that had appeared on the Earth. They surrounded and tormented. Ul'gen brought a flame and lit a fire. The evil spirits and vermin ran from the smoke of the fire and vanished. From that time onwards, and to this day, evil spirits are driven away using smoke.

The Shortsi, like many other peoples, believe in the duality of the human soul. The life of a human soul begins in the Upper World where it has no material form. Ul'gen sends it to the Earth as a sunbeam or a falling star and there it obtains material form. The soul may also come to Earth in the form of a 'bud-child' hanging like a leaf from the branch of a sacred birch tree.

These 'buds' are blown onto the earth by the kam (shaman). They are blown from the Upper World, to the head of the hearth. From there they reach into the woman's womb. The period in a person's life which occurs in the womb when the bones, body and blood are formed is also the time when a connection is made with the female, sky deity 'Umai'.

Humankind's earthly incarnation begins with the first breath, 'tin' and ends when the breath, 'tin' is cut short. Some believe that the soul leaves the body at the point of death and returns to the deity. Others believe that the soul leaves for the World of the Dead situated on the earthly plane, or that it moves on to the Under World.

The soul separates itself from the human body during sleep and takes the form of a small flame wandering from place to place and returning to the body when a person wakes. The Shortsi believe that the nostrils serve as the soul's entry and exit point. They say that if one places a piece of coal just in front of the nose the soul double will be too frightened to re-enter the nostrils and so the person won't awaken until the piece of coal falls off. Hunters feared that their soul may leave the body during sleep when they were out hunting and be caught by the mountain or taiga 'che ezi' (master spirit). Should a hunter lose his soul in this way he could fall ill and be forced to seek the help of a shaman on his return. (V. Potapov, 1991, p.29-30.)

The peoples of the Altai-Sayan region have a very specific understanding of the notion of 'soul' and the Shortsi are no exception. V. Verbitski lists six different terms referring to soul: tin, kut, tula, sune, sur, suzi. (Verbitski, 1893, 97-99) A.V.Anokhin mentions seven terms based on his notes on the Teleuti considering them all to represent different aspects of one integral 'soul'. He does not cite the term 'suzi' but adds the terms 'uzut' and 'jal salkyn' to Verbitski's list. (Funk, 1997, 196-218).

Most researchers note four main conditions of the soul referred to in Gornaya Shoriya:

1.'Tin-soul'. This condition is common to man, animals and plants and is the essential quality of breath which is lost upon death. 'Tin' is an integral element of all living beings. Verbitski expresses the notion clearly when he writes: "Tin is in fact lifelikeness..." (1893, 98).

The connection between life and breath could hardly have gone unnoticed when a child's life begins proper with the first breath and life ends with one's final exhalation. This explains the natural extension of the word 'tin' to plants and animals which were also all considered living, 'tinning', i.e. 'having breath'. Grass was considered 'tinning' until such time as it was either dug up and unearthed or mown. It is evident that the word 'tin' has a more extensive meaning than 'breath'. It expresses an understanding of life in a wider sense. The term 'tin bura' serves as an example of the wider semantics of the word 'tin'. 'Tin bura' was the name given to the animal the kam chose to carry him on his shamanic journeying and whose skin was wrapped around the drum. (Potapov, 1991, 32)

2. 'Kut-soul' pertains to man but also according to various sources, to animals and plants also. A person's health depends on 'kut' which is constantly under threat because 'kut' can be dragged into the lower world by the evil spirits 'aina', Erlik's helpers. Kut does not always necessarily occupy the body being absent during sleep (which is considered to be one's condition when 'kut' is journeying), loss of consciousness through fainting etc or in moments of extreme fright. In times of fear or great surprise kut sits in the back of the mouth. For this reason it was advised not to give oneself to extremes of these emotions. If kut leaves the body and is caught by 'aina' (evil spirits of te Lower World) then a person may fall ill. If 'aina' eat kut this causes the person's death. Kut is associated with a person's life-force from birth up until death. The loss of kut always leads to misfortune, be it in the form of illness or death. Of the deceased it is said; 'aina kutin chiibisti' – 'the aina ate his kut'. If a kam is able to retrieve kut, or in the rare instance that an aina returns a kut of its own accord, then a person may recover.

The presence of kut-soul serves as an indicator of life itself. Since this soul substance was created by Erlik, and it is considered that he has rights over it, Erlik may also choose for a lost kut to be returned to the body. This might be requested by a kam although Erlik is greedy and will agree to return a soul only in return for an exchange sacrifice. Before commencing a ceremony the kam looks into a cup containing 'araka' – 'milk spirit drink' and determines which particular 'aina' is tormenting the individual fallen ill. 'Aina' take various forms: 'Cher tegrize' is an earth spirit; 'Pashka tegri' is a 'foreign' spirit; 'Ejhik kormuze' is an invisible door spirit; 'Aalchi' is a vagrant spirit; 'Uzun-kormes' is a long invisible spirit; 'Ejhik ainazi' is a door spirit and 'Chebel nebe' a bad spirit. The last two are the most dangerous as they can consume the spirit not only of man but of cattle also. The kam is often unable to retrieve the soul taken by these two spirits and after the death of the victim it can be impossible to expel the aina (evil spirits) from the house which puts the other members of the household at risk too. One may be forced to leave the dwelling, completely remove household items and move to a new location. These spirits have been seen in the form of a tiny flame and have been heard dragging a soul along with them as they go. (Khlopina, 1992, p.136)

All the peoples of the Altai-Sayan region believe that kut-soul is given by a deity of the highest order and sent to earth in the form of a manifested 'embryo' of primordial life-force. The fire deity is also believed to take part in the transmission of kut. As a rule, when kut leaves the body of the deceased, it proceeds to the 'land of the dead'.

As concerns the kut of farm animals the same applies. They are received from one or another higher deity in the form of an embryo. Plant kuts however, are perceived slightly differently. It was generally believed that the kut of grass, herbs and cereals was found in the ground (olonnin kudi cherde Polcha) and had their origin in the spirits of the local valleys, forests, rivers, mountains and lakes. (Potapov. 1991, 35)

3. 'Surun eezi-soul'. This soul aspect pertains to humans only and immediately after death. When a person dies their kut leaves the body through the eyes and becomes 'Surun'. The 'surun eezi' soul aspect remains on the earth and wanders close to the home of the deceased or to those places where a person spent a great deal of time during their life. This 'wandering' may last for up to a year

or more after death. To prevent the soul from disturbing those still living in the home of the deceased, a ritual is carried out on the seventh day subsequent to the person's passing. A kam lights a fire in the house, ignites a small piece of kindling and smudges each member of the household three times. The kam takes the kindling out into the forest and throws it away in a forward direction. According to other sources such as L.P. Potapov and A.B. Anokhin the kam accompanies the 'surun' (departed soul) into the land of the dead along the downward flow of a nearby river on the fortieth day after passing. At this stage the soul aspect is referred to as 'uzut'.

4. 'Uzut-soul'. Uzut-soul is term given to the soul of the deceased after the fortieth day of passing. A year after death the uzut should leave for the realm of the deceased in the underworld once and for all. However, uzut does not always wish to leave, in this case preferring to remain on the earth. It is the role of the kam to persuade uzut to finally depart. Occasionally, uzut returns from the lower world on 'chukchan', the horse of the underworld. In this case the kam performs a ritual with a drum in order to force the uzut to leave again. During the 'kamlanie' (ritual) the kam communicates with the uzut-soul, whom it is given 'sees' more than the living. The uzut may communicate to the kam, who among the relatives will live long and who will fall ill or soon pass away, or give other advice. (Khlopina, 1992, 136)

The living were extremely wary of the dead and tried to avoid areas where burials were situated fearing to meet with the uzut-soul of a deceased - 'Uzut urunar'. If for some reason the passing rituals were not conducted at the appropriate times an uzut soul could turn into a truly evil spirit similar to an 'aina'. Such a spirit could be hostile and bring harm to its relatives.

In accordance with the model of the universe accepted by the Shortsi, the middle world, i.e. the world on the land, is populated by numerous spirit che ezi (master spirit of a place). Many researchers have put the worship of such spirits down to hunting cults, the attribution of soul to the natural environment and a spirit protector cult. There are ethical and moral codes connected with where one is situated within the natural world at any one time; be it in the taiga, in valleys or pasture lands, by rivers, lakes, mountain passes and at sacred mountains or within their proximity etc. The rules and behavioural codes for human presence in these places offer respect for the spirit che ezi of the given territory and reflect man's dependence on them. These rules and codes comprise of actions and prohibitions aimed at protecting the peace of the local spirit-che ezi, and their riches from man's intrusion.

The Shortsi also believe that a man's soul may be stolen by a mountain or water che ezi (master spirit). The mountain che ezi would take the form of a beautiful young woman who 'caught' a man with the intention of making him her husband. Folklore abounds with legends surrounding this motif. One such legend was told to us by the folkteller L.N. Arbachakova, (born 1930).

One day, three friends set out to go hunting. One of them always returned with a catch whilst the other two always returned empty handed. For three days they hunted and on the fourth day the two friends said to the third:

"There is no point in us continuing to hunt for nothing. We're going to turn home." Having said this, the two unlucky hunters set off home. The successful hunter remained. Once, in the evening, returning to his cabin after a day's hunting he was preparing his supper. Suddenly, he heard a person walk behind the cabin. The hunter decided that his two friends had returned. He walked out of the hut and looked around but could see no-one. He went back inside the hut and began to eat. Again, it seemed to him that someone stood in the doorway. Again he went outside to check but found no-one there.

He ate and finally lay down to sleep but as he lay he felt someone lie down beside him! He got up and walked around a little. When he was ready to lie down again he saw a figure sitting at the table. As he looked closer he saw that it was a beautiful woman who sat there. The hunter asked her:

"Who are you? Where have you come from?"

"I am the ezi (master spirit) of the mountain!" She replied.

"When in the autumn the mountain doors close, the ezi leave for the caves. Why did you not go?"

"I was delayed playing games and was late leaving for the cave. I have stayed to see the winter through. I have fallen in love with you and that's why I give you birds and game when you hunt. This winter I shall live with you and then in the spring when the doors of the mountain open we shall leave together for the cave. There we shall live together."

The hunter refused her offer and sent the girl away:

"Be away with you." He said.

In the days following he went hunting but returned empty handed. After a while the girl came to visit him again:

"I went to your lands and saw what your wife and cattle are like."

"How did you know where I live?" asked the hunter in surprise.

"We know everything," answered the girl, "let us marry and live together. You will suffer from nothing and I shall rid you of your wife."

Again the hunter refused. The girl wouldn't leave for a long time and then the hunter said:

"Let's go outside."

The hunter held back and then put a needle in a bullet and stabbed the girl in the back.

"What a villain you are," the girl cried. If you hadn't put the needle in the bullet then it wouldn't have reached me," she said weeping, and she walked away.

The hunter returned home thinking that now he would certainly catch nothing.

A year later he went hunting again in the same places as before. When he walked into the hut the same young woman came to him and said:

"You shot into me and I became pregnant and now you and I have a daughter. Come with me if you wish to see your daughter."

Together they set off in the direction of another mountain. The hunter looked and saw that there stood a beautiful girl somewhat similar to himself. The woman said:

"This is your daughter. Let us now live together!"

"I shall not leave my wife," answered the hunter, "I shall live with

Photo: Alexander Arbachakov

Mountains Shoria

you in the winter and go to my wife in the summer."

"In the summer I shall go with you too. I won't show myself to others. Only you shall see me."

The hunter refused and returned home. When he arrived he saw that everything was as it should be and that his wife was well. The next morning at breakfast however, his wife unexpectedly choked on some soured milk and died. At that moment the khozaika appeared and said:

"If you don't come and live with me you too shall die!"

The hunter again refused and the next morning, true enough, he also passed away. People said that he too had been 'eaten' by the khozaika of the mountain.

S.S. Torbokov, kaichi (throat singer and keeper of the oral history) and renowned Shor poet told of the magical effect of 'kai' (songs of the kaichi) on the mountain che ezi. When Shor hunters had arrived at a place where they intended to hunt they sprinkled milk on the ground (to appease the mountain spirit guardians). If there were a kaichi in their company they would organise for him to perform. In the hunter's cabin, sitting by the fire kai comes freely and easily and the kaichi would sing inspired by his surroundings. The kaichi sang to charm the mountain 'che ezi'.

All the 'che ezi' of various different mountains adore kai and in hearing it they become less attentive to watching over their animals and let them go free. These animals then become the hunter's bag.

The Shor also revere the water spirit as a powerful che ezi which is said to appear either in the form of a black horned animal or as a naked woman with long, golden hair.

In the spring, as soon as the ice began to melt and large pieces separate off and float with the current, a prayer meeting would be held. The village inhabitants, excluding the women, would gather at the side of the river bringing with them home-brewed beer and different kinds of food. Prayers and blessings were made and the libation ritual conducted. One or two individuals who knew how to make blessings were chosen for this role. Both poured beer into a large wooden cup which they would hold in their hands and sprinkle in the direction of the surrounding mountains and rivers praying for good food, for animals to be given at the hunt, and for there to be abundant fish in the rivers. The catch also depended on the water che ezi, 'sug eezi' which dwelt in the reaches of the river (koonu). After every prayer or request the two individuals would sprinkle some of the brew on the grass but always in the direction of the most prominent mountains and rivers.

The eldest village inhabitants remember times when the ritual 'shachyg', 'sprinkling offerings to the spirits', was conducted by a shaman. If there were no shaman in the village then the ritual could also be conducted by other village members. L.N. Arbachakova (born 1930) told us of how in Ust' Kabyrze this ritual was conducted early in the spring before the ice began to melt with the request that the ice melt well. Libation (ritual offering) was carried out in the direction of the mountains so that the animals and birds bred well. On the whole, rituals would be addressed to the mountains and rivers located in the immediate surrounding territory. For example, those living in Kabyrze addressed the mountain 'Kara Tag' and the Mrass and Pyzass rivers. 'Suga shachyglapchar: Chaksha parybyssyn, tep! Taga, an-kush chaksha ossun tep!'

Shog, shog, shog!
Great river!
Go well and quietly!
Shog, shog, shog!
Kara Tag Mountain
May the birds and animals
breed well!
Take no offense at our people!

(From a sound recording by L.N. Arbachakova)

O.N. Akulyakova, a villager from Chuvashka remembers the words that used to be spoken during libation to the spirits, (Shachyg taglarga, suglarga).

Large mountains
and small mountains,
Whose names and folknames
are unknown to me;
Large rivers
and small rivers,
Whose names and folknames
are unknown to me;
Be not offended.
Receive the offering I sprinkle you,
this sacred drink!

Before sending her son off to hunt or before driving her cattle to pasture O.N. Akulyakova would always make an offering to the spirits with the best alcoholic drink she had available. (Ashtyn shynygyn Ashtyn pashtapkudan urub-alyp.)

Be not offended
Mother Mrassu
If my son or cattle
Walk in your waters.

Cause them no ill
If they walk on the mountain
May they walk free from care,
My cattle (and son)!

Aside from Ul'gen and Erlik other deities particularly revered in the general cosmological system include Tegri, Cher-sug, and Ymai (Umai). These deities have enjoyed a prominent position among the Turkic peoples of Siberia from ancient times to the present day.

Of the ancient Turkic gods, the highest in the hierarchy was 'Tegri', the Sky god. The word 'Tegri' translates directly as 'sky'. During prayer and kamlanie the Shortsi similarly to other Altai-Sayan peoples attribute particular sacred meaning to the notion of 'Tegri'. The sky cult is one of the most widespread ancient cults in all of central Asia.

L.P. Potapov writes that this cult had been preserved until quite recently among the Khakas who conducted clan prayer meetings to the sky on the sacred mountain of Tigir-Tag right up until the late 1930's. Today the Shortsi do not practise the Tegri cult although in day to day life Tegri (sky god) may be made mention of as a sacred or higher essence: 'Tegri korcha' – 'The sky sees'. There are also practising Shor kam (shamans) (V.Ady'yakov and A.Kuspekova) who address the sky for assistance during kamlanie (ceremony).

It is interesting to note that many researchers have recorded that kam did not take part in the prayer meetings addressed to the sky. Normally such rituals were headed by revered elders, such as the heads of clans. The reason for this may be that Tegri-Sky was a higher deity than the kam and his spirit helpers had the right to address directly. Another explanation may be that the Tegri cult of the (sun), sky is a relic of the pre-shamanic faith Tengriism, widespread during the period of the Turkic Khaganate.

Prayers to the Sky took place on a gentle slope near the top of a sacred mountain. A series of prohibitions were associated with this mountain with the aim of protecting it from sacrilege. The well known Mustag (Pistag) mountain in the Tashtagolsk region represents one such sacred ritual mountain. Almost all the kam with whom we met said that Mustag Mountain was where the most important spirits dwelled and that kam received their spirits and power there.

Unfortunately, Mustag has today been turned into a place for recreation with ski runs, cable cars and a Slavonic church cross has been erected on one of its peaks. No consultation was made with the local indigenous population before these activities were undertaken. One may draw parallels with the story of the shrine to Christ the Saviour which the Bolsheviks tore down and built a swimming pool in its place. One wonders whether history has taught humankind anything at all.

The second most important notion or name to be used by kam and which is cited in ethnographic literature by a number of researchers is 'Cher-Sug' which translates as 'Earth-Water'.

V.V. Radlov describes this term as an independent deity. Quoting his field research: 'The expression 'd'arsu' or 'd'ar-sub' in reference to a deity is still used by the Altai, Teleut and Shortsi who practise shamanism.' It would seem that at that time the two cults of Cher-Sug and Ul'gen existed simultaneously among the Altaitsi, Teleuti and Shortsi.

These peoples personify the deity 'Cher-Sug' with the Earth, (Mother-Earth, Ezi of the Earth). The Teleuti, Shortsi and Khakassi share the same perception of Cher-Sug as the main Earth spirit, which according to the established hierarchy of deities: rules over all the earth spirits, mountain, forest, rock and river guardians.

It is hardly surprising that the Shortsi along with the other Turkic peoples of Altai-Sayan attributed a deity to the most important event in a person's life; their birth. This deity is referred to as 'Umai'. When translating ancient runic inscriptions (the monument to Kyul' Tegin) V.V. Radlov marked the understanding of Umai as 'goddess-protector' and made reference to the Shortsi, who refer to the guardian of young children and spirit accompanier of the deceased, with the same name. Potapov records the Shor tradition of digging a place near the hearth to hide a child's umbilical chord (ymai) wrapped in birch bark. The word 'ymai' was given both to the umbilical chord and navel and also to the deity who acted as the protector of newborn children.

Shortsi from the Chelei clan explain difficult births as the battle between an 'aina' (evil spirit) who stands at the pregnant mother's feet trying to steal the child's 'kut-soul' and the ezi 'Umai' who stands at her head trying to pull the 'kut' towards her to save it. If the baby lived then Umai had succeeded and the child was placed under her protection. If the 'aina' won then the child died.

V. Verbitskii confirms the existence of the Umai deity among the Shortsi, giving two meanings of the word in his dictionary: 'Kind spirit, protector of small children; Angel of death.' The second meaning could refer to the evil spirit 'Kara-Umai' who took the lives of small children.

In worship of 'Umai', the Shortsi prepared bows and arrows for boys and spindles for girls as protective amulets. These were attached close to the cradle and regularly 'fed' with 'talkhan'*, cedar nuts or 'shalyg' (dried meat).

L.P. Potapov believes that the ancient Turkic Goddess 'Umai' was through time transformed into the cult of spirit guardian of the natural world among the Altai peoples - in which he included the Shortsi. Among the ancient Turkic people 'Umai' was a highly revered, female deity considered protector of the Turkic people as a whole, whereas the peoples of the Altai-Sayan consider 'Umai' to be protector only of mothers and their young children.

* 'Talkhan' – is a food of a flour consistency made of fried barley seeds and ground. It is added to tea, milk or mixed with water and cream.

WHO IS THE KAM?

The word 'shaman' first appears in dispatches sent by Russian ministers from Siberia in the seventeenth century who adopted the term from the Tungus. As a result the word 'shaman' was used to denote the servers of the cult of the Siberian native peoples and the ritual actions themselves became known as 'shamanism'.

The Siberian peoples have their own word, however, which corresponds to the word 'shaman': Among the Turkic peoples of the Altai-Sayan territory including the Shortsi, the mediator between man and the spirit world is referred to as 'kam'.

The Shortsi believe that the kam is chosen by the spirits. It was not possible to become a kam of one's own choosing. The function of being mediator between the different worlds, between man and the spirits was given from on high by Ul'gen. The sign of a kam was an 'extra bone' (artyk sook). This could be a sixth finger or a protuberance on a hand or foot.

I.D. Khlopina writes that in earlier times when a child was found to have such a sign the advice of a kam was sought. The kam in turn took advice from the spirits to determine whether the child would become a kam or not. If it was decided that the child would indeed become a kam then it was instilled in them from childhood that they were a shaman.

The passing of spirit-helpers from one kam to another took place in the following way: After the death of a kam the spirits descended into the under world realm of Erlik and stayed there until the time came for the inheritor to practise kamlanie (shamanic ritual). From time to time Erlik would send his spirits onto the earth to find the one chosen by Ul'gen. When the individual had been located, Erlik would send them an 'aina'

Photo: Alexander Arbachakov

Contemporary Siberian Shor Village

spirit carrying an illness. The chosen individual would fall ill as a result with the so-called 'shamanic illness'. The future shaman would continue to be ill until they consciously accepted their role as shaman. Often, a practising shaman would be called for healing. But in learning of the true cause of the illness the shaman could refuse to give the healing lest Erlik become angry and punish them.

During the phase of illness the future kam would begin communicating with the spirits. The spirits would come to him or her in dreams and delirium. The illness could last for a long time possibly up to three years. A kam would visit the shaman to be and begin teaching them how to conduct ritual kamlanie. As soon as the kam began communicating with the spirits the illness would fall away. The first communication takes place with the fire spirit 'ot eezi', then with the mountain sprit Pistag (Mustag) and then with Erlik. (Khlopina, 1992, p.138)

N.A. Alekseev gives a description of kam, Feofan's, illness from Ust'Mrass published by N.P. Dyrenkova. During his illness Feofan saw a spirit similar to a person who 'took him into the taiga and dragged him through the water. The kam thought he would choke and drown and then something began to press down on him and it became unbearably stuffy. The spirit persuaded Feofan to become a kam and told him of the worlds above and below the ground. The spirit promised to help him. There were times when he ordered him to do a kamlanie, threatening him with death if he refused. For a long time Feofan resisted and suffered from his illness all that time. When he finally began to practise shamanism his illness fell away." (N.A. Alekseev, 1984, p.134)

Almost all shamans go through the period of so-called 'shaman's illness'. The kam we were able to meet with and whose kamlanie are described here, all told us of how they suffered this illness before becoming practising kam.

Sometimes, shamanic ability is inherited. Sensing that death is near a kam may pass his spirits on to a son, daughter or grand-child if they have the 'extra bone', 'artyk sook'. Among the Shortsi, however, it was not necessarily considered desirable for there to be a new kam in the family. The previous kam's drum and rattle were taken into the forest and hung from a young birch tree and the house was rid of all their possessions. If on the other hand the presence of a new kam in the family was welcomed, then a relic or flinder from the old kam's drum were stuffed into a crack of the old barn wall which no-one was supposed to touch. (Khlopina, 1992, 138)

So either by right of inheritance, or by surviving the 'shaman's illness', the kam acquired his spirit-helpers. In either case, each kam had their personal spirit-helpers.

L.P Potapov defines two categories of spirit: spirit protectors and spirit-helpers. The spirit protectors were usually deities or spirits of high rank such as Ul'gen or his sons, the fire deity or the che ezi (master spirit) of a sacred mountain. Spirit protectors would come to the kam's assistance either at his request or in response to a prayer or sacrifice.

Spirit helpers are divided into two categories. The first are 'tos', the ancestral spirits, particularly the spirits of those who were themselves previously kam. The second are those serving spirits which the kam summons through the drum beat in kamlanie ritual. (Potapov, 1991, 65)

L.P. Potapov considers the fire (deity) spirit, 'ot eezi' to belong to the category of protector spirits and believes this deity to represent part of an ancient heritage. Kam begin their kamlanie by making offerings to 'eezi'. The fire spirit in particular served not only as the kam's protector but also as mediator for communication with deities of a higher rank. (Potapov, 1991, 66) Earlier, it was considered a sacrilege to throw rubbish on the fire, place sharp metal objects near the fire, step over the fireplace or stand on the ashes. Both contemporary shamans and the most elderly generation still revere the spirit of the fire. Olimpiada Nikolaevna Akulyakova remembers that when an offering of fat was made to the fire 'che ezi', the following words were spoken:

Odys tabyrlyg? ot enem!	Mother-fire with thirty tongues!
Kyryk tostig, kys enem!	Mother-maiden, mountain mother spirit!
Akcy-purnun chagbanzyn!	May your centre always be still!
Chag shajha percham!	Receive my offering of lard!
Kyiryk chap korbezin!	May you see no unrest!
Kyiryk-chabal artyk kelbezin!	May conflict pass us by!
Kebege-eezi emni kadarzyn!	May the *che ezi* of the fire guard our home!

The kam's high guardians are the che ezi of the sacred mountain that give the shaman his drum and in honour of which special prayer meetings were held. The spirit of the sacred mountain would observe that the kam conducted the kamlanie and other rituals properly and could punish him for not observing the necessary conditions.

Whereas Ul'gen, Erlik, the fire, and sacred mountain spirits act as protectors who may come to the kam's assistance from time to time or keep an eye on him - there are other spirit helpers who do the kam's 'dirty work', if one can put it that way. N.A. Alekseev emphasizes that 'the Shortsi believe that Ul'gen attributes the shaman spirit with helpers from among those spirits that dwell in the upper world. Some shamans believe that their spirits live in the nine rungs leading to Ul'gen. The stronger spirits dwell higher up and the weaker lower down. Spirit-helpers could also represent beings belonging to the middle world such as reptiles,

frogs, lizards and snakes that live in the river and the fire.' (Alekseev, 1984, c.89)

Whether a kam was judged to be powerful or weak depended on his spirit-helpers. The spirits of a powerful shaman were considered more potent than the spirits of a weak shaman.

As a rule a shaman would have five, seven or nine spirit-helpers, 'toster'. A shaman with nine spirits would be the most powerful even being capable of devouring people. A shaman with only three spirits was considered the weakest.

Photo: Llyn Roberts

Bridge in Shor Territory

The spirits of deceased shamans (tos) similarly to the spirits of the mountains, forests and valleys are attributed to the category of earth spirits because they stay on the earth after death rather than moving into the 'land of the dead'. Many kam who, in addition to their unusual gift have also inherited spirit-helpers, know of their unusual genealogy. These kam are considered of high birth and are particularly revered. For all kam one of the most important spirits is the spirit of the drum which is called 'the drum che ezi' or 'ezi'. The drum was the most important ritual attribute and demonstrated to all that the owner belonged to a small number of those chosen from above. The permission to use the drum was granted by the higher spirit-deities or the 'che ezi' of the sacred mountain. Among the Shor the handle symbolised the spirit of the drum which took the form of a rod, widening at the ends. L.P.Potapov emphasizes that the drum was the kam's most important attribute, more important than the ritual garb, for example. Repeating one of the earliest descriptions of a Shor drum was written by the German researcher 'Iogann-Georg Gmelin who spent time with the Abintsi in the year 1734: "...We called for a kam who was going to conduct a ritual. He brought a drum with him which looked something like a sieve with one side covered in leather. On the hollow side a wooden rod was attached than ran vertically through the centre. In the middle where the kam held the drum the rod was thinner, moving into two goblet shapes, supposedly to intensify the sound, on either side of the hand and then tapering out again at the edges where the cross piece meets the frame. Both ends were triple-sided. Perpendicular to the wooden handle an iron rod is fixed on each side of which hang five hollow iron flinders. This rod runs horizontally, not through the middle but off centre and therefore is not held in the hand. The rattle is a flinder, removed and re-sewn in hare skin and decorated in ribbons and strings. (Gmelin, 1994, p.13)

Among the Shortsi the kam wouldn't make their drum. This seems linked with the earlier idea that a new kam was chosen by an elder kam relative who made the drum. Likewise, a new drum could not serve for ritual purposes until it had been 'brought alive'.

Before receiving their drum the kam could carry out rituals using a glove, a small broom, a hat or an old bow. A kam who was still weak was called 'shabynchi'. A weak kam or a kam who was just learning could heal the sick, drive out 'aina', stop the rain, or clear the clouds. At the present time there are no shamans in Gornaya Shoriya who use a drum. This is partly because so many rituals and traditions were lost during the Soviet period when an anti-religious battle was fought. Those individuals who decided to continue practising shamanism did not wish to draw attention to themselves so they refrained from using a drum, even if they had the power to do so. Normally they made do with a

Shaman's Drum

towel or small broom. In answer to our enquiries we were told that there were no individuals left now who could make a drum properly, observing all the rituals and who could subsequently bring the drum to life.

I.D. Khlopina cites the example of a simple kamlanie to clear the rain: 'It had been raining since morning. Today there will be 'baiga', a wedding celebration with the meal outside. The rain threatens to spoil the event. The female kam 'Keklek' was called from the same village. She began the kamlanie at seven in the morning. No-one was allowed to smoke as the smoke drives the spirits away. She carried out the ritual without a drum which isn't necessarily required to clear the rain clouds. She used a bow and sat on a low bench near the hearth. She pulled back the bow and tweaked the bowstring. Along with the speed of her movements the spirits (tos) began to gather to her. The kamka began to shake and then she shook harder. Her head twitched and she began to give out hoarse noises as if pushing them out of her stomach. Then she began to pronounce different words, at times compre-hensible and at others times seemingly without meaning. She addressed the threatening rain clouds 'kek-nulut' and persuaded them to leave. The sky did indeed clear. (Kamka Keklek. Pyzas, sook Kechin, August 1927)' (Khlopina, 1992.p.136)

Before making the drum the 'orba'- 'rattle' was made. Members of the kam's clan took part in making the rattle. A branch of meadow-sweet (tamylga) was taken, wrapped in cloth and sewn with hemp thread or horse hair in a piece of white hare skin. The tail piece of an 'ak-kiik', (Northern deer) was sewn to the head scarf as a sign that the kam's motives and actions would be pure and white and therefore the spirits would be benevolent towards him. Members of the clan tied ribbons to one end of the 'orba' and a leather loop to the other end which the kam put his hand through during kamlanie. If the kam were to drop the 'orba' during kamlanie then all the spirits would disperse and disappear 'abyrtka' (liquid barley malt ritual offering) prepared beforehand was poured into three 'kuspak', (large, birch-bark containers) which were placed in an open clearing next to a bench or stool. The kam would sit and begin to 'kamlat', beating the rattle on his palm. The sacred mountain Pistag (Mustag) would convey to the kam whether Ul'gen had given permission for a drum to be made and for the kam to be the drum's master (always of the male line). A specific time would be indicated for the drum's preparation, usually in spring or autumn, and it would also be specified how the drum should be made and from which specific materials. For example, the instructions may be: beside a particular river, close to a particular stone grows a willow. From this tree the drum hoop should be made; in a particular place (given in detail) a bird cherry grows from which the drum's outer hoop should be made. These trees would be situated far from the village where neither dogs nor cattle wander. The kam had to fell these trees himself and bring them to his home. Pistag would also determine (communicate to the kam) who should make the hoop. It was also dictated which birch be used for the handle; where the birch grew; which images should be executed on it and what should be used to draw them, such as the fine bones of a hazel-grouse. It was also conveyed who should make the iron rod with the hangings. After all these instructions had been received the kam sprinkled 'arbytka' (barley malt offering) in the direction of Pistag and asked its ezi for all to go well in the preparation of the drum. Then those present would drink 'arbytka' and disperse.

Approximately one week before the stipulated time, preparations were made for the sacred actions: 'tuur apparchigan' was the receiving the drum, and 'tuur-toi' was the drum celebration. All members of the clan prepared for the general celebration. (Khlopina, 1992, p.138)

According to informants N.A. Alekseev and I.D. Khlopina the

drum was prepared in the following way: 'The drum was made by several individuals. One made the hoop. This individual found the willow marked by Ul'gen, sawed off the size of wood needed and planed it with a scraper – 'adylga' which is used for carving out boats. From this piece a thin board was made and then soaked in the river until it became flexible. A hole was then burned and drilled out at both ends and the board bent into a circle or oval shape sixty to seventy centimetres in diameter. The ends were held together and thin straps of horse hide sewn through the holes. The finished loop was taken to the kam on the eve of the drum kamlanie. For added strength the drum frame was covered with two thin hoops made from fine bird-cherry branch. On the outer surface of the upper section (where the diagram of the world was drawn) five small columns were attached carved from birch growth. These formed the drums 'lips' or 'brows'. The handle piece was made of a birch bar and attached to the inner hoop. The image of the drum's che ezi (master spirit) 'tor-oz' was carved out at both ends of the rod with bronze shiny nails knocked in, serving as eyes. Between these two carved images scorched hazel-grouse bones were attached as ornaments. The finished handle was also taken to the kam on the eve of the kamlanie. Once at the kam's house, the ends of the handle piece were slightly sharpened and in accordance with their diameter openings were burned and cut into the longitudinal edges of the outside hoop into which the ends of the hand piece were fitted. Along one edge, a row of holes was burned into the width of the frame, each hole being thirty-five centimetres apart. Hemp thread was then wound through the holes and passed through loops of soft willow, attached firmly to the opposite side of the drum. All birch and willow off cuts were burned.

A blacksmith would forge a fine bar with small protuberances necessary so that the attached hangings would hold in place and not slip down the bar. The bar, called 'Temir kirish', was fixed into the opening on the rim alongside the handle piece and hangings were attached such as bells, metal, twisted plates, hollow tubes and strips of material in various colours. The number of hangings, called 'sunmyr' or 'kylysh', usually corresponded to the number of the kam's spirit-helpers. The spirit-helpers are normally ruled by Erlik but can also be at the disposal of a spirit above the earth. The function of the 'sunmyr' (hangings) is to guard the spirit-helpers from the evil spirits 'aina'. Above the crosspiece on both sides of the handle three metal hangings were attached called 'sabres' or 'swords'.

Several weeks previous to the kamlanie a member of the clan would bring the skin of a wild goat, Siberian deer or stag killed in the taiga. The skin was soaked in the river attached to the bank by ropes until the fur could be scraped off easily. The day before the kamlanie, the skin was spread on a wooden board. One end was attached to the ground and the other held in the hands. Having scraped off all the fur the hide was placed on the ground and rinsed with several buckets of water. The skin was then thrown over a fence or other convenient construction and pulled hard by several individuals from both ends.

After this procedure was complete the drum frame was placed on the ground outside the kam's home and covered with the skin which was pulled and fixed securely to the drum. The ropes were tightened with the help of a stick whilst all the time the skin was pulled downwards to keep the tension. At the same time two or three helpers would stand over the drum spreading the skin out and smoothing its surface. When the skin was clearly spread well to the frame, the drum was turned over and the excess skin cut away with a knife leaving just a few centimetres width was left from the edge of the frame.

This procedure was usually finished towards the evening. Then a fire would be lit and several individuals would take turns to smoke the drum over the fire turning it quickly. Two others would stand to the sides and beat the drum constantly with birch and the smoking of the drum would often continue all night. (Alekseev. 1991, p.169; Khlopina, 1992, p.140-41).

Sacred images were executed on the outside of the drum skin. Symbolic images were drawn in the upper section which would include representations of the heavenly bodies, stars and other supernatural objects like the Sacred birch and poplar trees and the milky lake. According to the Shor worldview the kam's birch reaches high up into the clouds and there connects with two parallel, silk threads leading to the heavenly spheres as if the kam climbed up the birch and threads on his journeying. (Alekseev, 1984. p.169)

In addition to the celestial images the kam's spirit-helpers were also drawn in the upper section. Every kam had a specific number of spirit-helpers depending on his power. This part of the drum also carried images of the mythical animal 'bura' who served as the kam's 'steed' on his journeys to Ul'gen. Above all, the drum served as the kam's 'mount'. In the animistic world view of the Shortsi, the spirit or soul of the animal - 'chula' - whose skin had been wrapped around the drum, stayed with the drum and represented one of the kam's main spirit helpers. The strip across the middle separated the upper and lower parts of the drum and symbolically the Upper World and the Earth, 'Cher'.

In the lower half of the drum skin, images of the drum rattle 'orba', spirit che ezi, and a spirit firing an arrow at evil spirits were drawn. Horses for the journey to Erlik, the mythical animal 'Ker-Bos', and spirits in the form of reptiles, frogs, snake and lizard were also included in this section.

According to the images on the kam's drum one could determine his status or power. One could tell immediately whether the kam had the right to address Ul'gen and whether he was able to descend into the Under World during kamlanie.

Once the drum was finished it had to be brought to life. Representing a sacred object of huge symbolic meaning the drum also required social sanctioning during its ritual making by the kam's fellow clan members, which lasted for several days. In bringing the drum to life, the animal whose skin had been used in the making was also brought to life. The drum was finally displayed to the High Spirit or deity for approval and recognition of its suitability for kamlanie. After this stage the drum became a sacred object which could be used by the kam alone. From this moment onward, the kam's future life would be intimately connected with the drum. The deity would also communicate how many years the kam would use this particular drum and how many drums he would need in his lifetime.

In 1927 I.D. Khlopina described the ritual of 'bringing the drum to life':

"From the next morning preparations for the kamlanie began. The men present each gave the kam a strip of material or coloured 'chalaba' either on behalf of the family or several clan members and attached them to the iron bar of the drum. First nine strips were attached signifying the nine 'tos', the mountain che ezi that are passed on the road to Ul'gen. The strips symbolise clothes for the 'tos', the kam's helpers. Then a clearing is chosen nearby the house. Either seven or nine 'kuspak' (birch containers for 'abyrtka', barley malt offering) are brought depending on the number of specified mountains. 'Abyrtka' is made by the village members and the apparatus used to make the 'araka' (spirit drink) is placed nearby for preparation if the drink has not been prepared previously. Two or three young birch are taken from the forest and fixed in the ground close to the birch containers and propped up using pegs. Nine wedges are chopped out of each birch signifying the nine steps to Ul'gen through the nine mountains. The birch is the ladder the kam uses to climb up into the ninth sky. The new drum and rattle and sometimes the kam's clothes also are hung on one of the birch trees.

Several 'terbish', flat boxes similar in shape to a deep tray, are also made from birch bark. At a distance from the clearing, women knead dough from flour and water. Several fire rings are constructed from stones and large cooking pans placed on top. 'Tertpek', small bread buns, are boiled and placed in the 'terbish' (trays) and then put alongside the 'araka' (spirit drink) containers. Beside them, a low bench or stool - 'utlanchak' - is placed, also made of birch. Such are the preparations for the ritual.

At the first kamlanie, Ul'gen communicates to the kam how many times in his life he must change his drum and in how many years time. For example, the kam Stepan has worked as a kam for thirty five years and changed his drum after three, four, six and eight years. The kam Sachin from Bezas village practised shamanism for three years. Knowing how long he will use each drum for kamlanie, the kam may estimate also how long he will live.

At the same time, a horse is prepared for sacrifice. The kam begins the kamlanie with his new drum, beating it with his hand. He sits on the 'utlanchak' (birch stool) and recounts his journey to Ul'gen, describing the animal tracks he sees which will be abundant in winter and the paths he takes which will be best for hunting. He describes his journey through the Golden Lake (Lake Teletskoe) and the Golden Comb (Atyn mergen range)'. On the way he visits the mountain che ezi (master spirit) along the Mrass and at the Ust'-Kabyrza, Azyr, Kichik-Gelen, Taiga, Ulug-Gelen and Shakchak villages. He visits the fire che ezi 'ot eezi' and at this point one of those present takes a stick sharpened at one end from one of the fixed birches (ala-azak, 'the many coloured leg'), lights the stick in the fire and approaches the kam. The kam raises the drum up high and tosses it upwards as a gesture that he is beginning to approach Ul'gen (Upper World deity) and moving through the first and then subsequent levels of the sky. The individual who has approached the kam with the lighted stick then circles the drum with it three times saying the words, 'alas, alas'. Those present repeat the words 'alas, alas' (alas, alastarga – bless, glorify). The ritual element of circling the drum with a small torch is called 'alastapcha, tudun ishtepcha' which means smudging - using smoke to bless. The last mountain to be passed is Shakchak, after which the kam begins his journey through the sky. The final animal tracks to be noted by him are those of the 'sable'." (Khlopina, 1992, p.141)

During her research N.P. Dyrenkova recorded details of the ritual 'courting' of the drum and the subsequent 'marriage'. The essence of the courting is analogous to the drum 'enlivening' ritual except that the forms and scenario differ slightly. Once the drum is made the kam visits the home of the drum maker to court his drum. The drum spirit ezi should become his 'wife'. The 'bride's' 'mother' and 'father', i.e. the drum makers - place the new drum close to them tying it in a ladies head scarf and receiving the kam's relatives. Whilst the 'father' is being made offerings either the kam himself or a relative steals the drum and flees the house. Scandalous scenes are played out after which all are offered 'araka'. Folklore has it that the ezi of the drum would show herself to the kam only three drums later in his practise. The drum ezi took the form of a girl, short in height, with a family of combs and necklaces consisting of the hangings which had been attached to the drum. After the 'courting' the kam conducted the kamlanie of his journey to Ul'gen. The higher deity would inspect the drum and convey the period of its use and how many more drums the kam would require during his life time. This kamlanie was called 'the wedding'.

The drum fulfilled a variety of ritual functions. As mentioned above, the drum symbolised the mount the kam used during his search for the necessary spirits. If during the search the kam came across a water boundary then the drum served as a boat. If the kam met with evil spirits then during his battle with them the drum became a bow, firing arrows at the enemies. Among the Turkic peoples of the Altai-Sayan including the Shortsi, the drum also represented the object of a particular cult. It served as a universal model for the relationship between humans and the surrounding world. In his analysis of different kinds of shamanic drum L.P. Potapov writes: "this study of shamanic drums should be concluded by emphasizing their role as an essential and very specific sacred object within Altai shamanism. The drum combines information on theology and cult ritual at the same time as representing a valuable source for the study and knowledge of religion."

Aside from the drum, the ritual garb worn only by the kam represents an essential shamanic attribute yet unlike other Turkic peoples, the Shor kam did not use specific clothing. This fact has been noted by almost all researchers of Gornaya Shoriya. Normally the kam wore a new, light coloured kaftan called a 'shabur' modestly decorated with ribbons.

I.D. Khlopina wrote: 'The kam is sewn new clothes always from white coarse linen and bought a new white head scarf. In some areas like Bezas on the Kondom the new clothes are put on before the kamlanie and in other areas they are hung on a birch and when they have been symbolically received from Ul'gen they are put on immediately after the kamlanie." (Khlopina, 1992, p.142)

S.E. Malov writes that the Shor shamanic clothing consists of 'Shabur', a white coarse linen material and a hat with feathers from the tail of an eagle owl. If there was no hat a white headscarf was used also fixed with feathers. (Malov, 1909, p.39). N. P. Dyrenkova also shows evidence of the Shor kam using birch bark caps in their kamlanie to Ul'gen.

L.P.Potapov notes that bunches of owl feathers were attached to the linen kaftan in which the kam conducted his ceremonies. More often than not the kaftan differed from everyday wear in that the collar was decorated with coloured thread embroidered in a simple pattern. Whatever other symbolic meaning the embroidery might have it gave the kaftan the look of a special occasion appropriate for the kam to meet with the deities or spirits during kamlanie. (Potapov, 1991, p.208)

We in turn may confirm this particular characteristic of Shor kam clothing. During our meetings with kam and recordings of their kamlanie only Akulina Kuspekova specially dressed in a white kaftan which we suspected might be a medical coat and covered her head in a light-coloured headscarf.

SHOR SHAMANIC RITUALS

Each 'kamlanie' (ritual or ceremony) has a specific purpose. In his analysis of Altai shamanism, L.P. Potapov defines the main functions of 'kamlanie'. Besides those already mentioned (healing, journeying to other worlds and divination) he includes: kamlanie of one's enemy, changing the weather and participation in funeral rites.

Shaman's Bride

Artist: Luba Arbachakov

N.A. Alekseev observes that every Shor clan had its own figures who conducted traditional rituals and despite the attempts made to convert the population to Christianity, shamanism retained its position. N.P. Dyrenkova states that kamlanie is conducted at all major events in an individual's life such as at a difficult birth or at death, accompanying the soul of the deceased into the next world. Rituals could be conducted at times of success and of those of misfortune. A kamlanie could mark a successful hunt or an abundant harvest. First and foremost however, the main responsibility of the shaman was to heal the sick.

In turn, we note that to the present day it is quite customary for the Shortsi to turn to a shaman for healing, to predict the near future, and to find a lost animal be it a cow or a horse – as well as for the healing of these animals.

During our expeditions we recorded what is in our view an extremely interesting type of 'kamlanie' called 'Journey to the Deserted Churt', -'Eski Churt'*- which may be described as a conversation between the shaman and an individual's ancestral spirits.

We have already mentioned the example of 'kamlanie' being used to effect the weather and stop the rain described by I.D. Khlopina. This type of kamlanie is still widespread in Gornaya Shoriya and the authors had the opportunity to witness this ritual on numerous occasions. This kamlanie is most often conducted at haymaking time when poor weather can have a severe effect on the process of preparing fodder for cattle. Normally, one of the elders takes a rake and speaks an incantation requesting that the rain clouds pass the place by. When speaking the incantation the elder shakes his head, spits in the direction of the rain clouds and then drops the rake on the ground quite abruptly as if shoving some-one away.

The shaman's most important function, however, is to heal the sick. The Shortsi believe that illness arises when a person's 'kut-soul' has left the body for some reason and is unable to find its way back. The soul may simply have lost its way or have been taken by evil spirits. Before beginning a healing the kam makes a diagnosis to determine the reason for the illness. After the diagnosis the kam immediately begins the healing. Each kam has their own set of spirits and depending on the type of kamlanie being performed the kam calls various spirits to him. Spirit-helpers may be given instructions and spirit guardians and protectors asked for assistance. The spirits help to relocate the lost soul which the kam then returns to the individual by blowing their lost 'kut' in through the ears.

If a person is only slightly unwell the kam may read an incantation and conduct a small kamlanie as if driving out the evil spirit and their ill intentions. In the case of a more serious illness a longer kamlanie would be required possibly lasting all night. During the kamlanie the kam journeys into the other worlds to catch the evil spirit (aina) or to 'pay' the higher beings for the return of the person's health. The process ends with the disbandment of the spirit helpers and a divination regarding the results of the healing.

N.A. Alekseev records that the colourful incantations sometimes verging on wonderful, poetic works confirm the power of the kam's spirit helpers and describe the difficult battle that takes place to save or protect someone fallen ill. During kamlanie shamans genuinely communicate with invisible beings and visit their 'dwelling places'. In conducting a ritual the shaman may fall into a trance or ecstatic state, losing consciousness. (Alekseev, 1984, p.199)

The kam played one of the most important roles at a funeral. The relatives would deal with the preparation of the body and burial and the kam would fulfill other functions. The kamlanie would take place during the wake or at a later date at the time when it became essential to accompany the soul of the deceased to the land of the dead once and for all.

L.P Potapov considers that the perception of death and existence of the deceased in the afterlife clearly reveals a belief in the 'double'. All Turkic peoples including the Shortsi believe that the dead continue to live in the 'other land' and there go about their usual activities such as farming and hunting. Certain hunters believe that their deceased relatives and ancestors hunted in the mountains of 'Kuznetskogo Alatau' and that at times their shots can still be heard. Ritual conversations with the deceased, conducted whilst making offerings to the fire were held on specific days after the funeral.

Among the Shortsi of the lower reaches of the Mrassu River, on the fortieth day after death a shaman would call the deceased into the home where relatives and close friends were present. The deceased would come to bid them farewell and would weep, expressing their distress at the parting. The shaman would imitate the voice of the deceased and then address them directly: "Now I shall lead you away." Then the shaman, accompanied by the relatives, would go out to a sacred birch tree just beyond the village where they parted with the souls of the deceased.

These rituals were called 'kojhug' - 'migrations'. If the deceased were a man then the shaman conducted the ritual holding an axe. In the case that the deceased was a woman the shaman held a trowel, 'ozun'. At the end of the kamlanie these objects were thrown under the tree and then the villagers returned to their homes. The items left under the tree were to be touched by no-one and left completely alone. (Potapov, 1991, p.155)

I.D. Khlopina quotes a rough text of a kamlanie conducted at a 'Kojhug' (migration of the soul):

Uzut: (soul of the deceased) "I died not of my will. I died and that is how it has remained."

Kam (shaman): "Yes, you died not of your will. That is how it was."

Uzut: "My life was just so short."

Kam: "That is how he created it and so that is why you died."

Uzut: "Dark years have come into my life. I am separated from the light of day and go to the place of the dead. How mournful that light has remained and I have died. May those I leave behind, live peacefully" (Khlopina, 1992, p.137)

Divination and prediction is a very widespread and popular function of kamlanie. People turn to this form of kamlanie when they wish to determine the sex of an unborn child or confirm whether they will have success in hunting. It should be noted that divination and prediction were not necessarily always carried out by a kam. Almost every ulus (village) had its 'official' diviners - 'arbyshchi'. Both kam and 'arbyshchi' however, used similar methods and attributes which included water, stones and pulse-reading. During our expeditions we, the authors, had the oppor-tunity to experience pulse-reading ourselves. Having read the person's pulse the kam would then look for a long time into their eyes. Then she or he would describe the person's character, the main events in their life and predict their near future.

* 'Churt' - means dwelling or settlement inhabited by a single clan

THE LAST OF THE SHOR SHAMANS

During 1994-2003 we were fortunate to record thirteen ritual kamlanie from seven different kam. Six kamlanie are versions of 'Eski Churt' (connection between kam and person's ancestral spirits), 'The Deserted Churt'; one kamlanie is a version of 'The Soul Catch'; two kamlanie are versions of 'Home Cleansing'; three of 'Healing the Sick'; one of 'The Deceased'; and one of 'Aalas Lyube'. The texts of two recordings of the kamlanie 'Eski Churt', 'The Deserted Churt', are included in this book. These texts are taken from recordings of K.P. Chudekov and A.A. Tudegesheva. Here, we include the biographical details of contemporary shamans that we consider to be of ethnographic value.

All the kam we conversed with said that before beginning to practise shamanism they suffered from the 'shaman's illness' and that at the point when they started to practise shamanism their illness passed.

In addition to the drum, the following attributes were used during ritual: 'shorbu' (a bunch of small birch branches), towel (a head scarf, shawl or other piece of material) and a rough working glove filled with sand, clay or ashes. All the kam conducted the kamlanie in their everyday clothes as they have no special ritual garb. However, we noticed that on our second visit to Akulina Kuspekova in the summer of 2002, she changed into a white house coat and tied her hair in a light head scarf especially for the kamlanie.

Before conducting the ritual 'Eski Churt', the kam always asked about the location and surname of the family in question. On learning the name of L.N. Arbachakova's home village, kam K.P. Chudekov said that he had been there before and so it would not be difficult for him to journey there. (The shaman's journey takes place on the mental plane with the assistance of the spirit-helpers.)

In addition to kamlanie most of these kam can 'pulse read', 'Kol tudarga' which means literally 'to hold the hand'. By the beat of the pulse the kam can determine a person's character and predict their future.

All our recordings were made of kam living in the Tashtagolskii rayon in the Kemerevo region. Many of them, already being in declining years when they were recorded, are sadly no longer with us.

Evdokiya Gavrilovna Todyyakova

Evdokiya Gavrilovna Todyyakova (maiden name Labysheva) was born in 1927 in Labysh village, (Klyuchevskoi village soviet, Tashtagol'skii region). At the present time she lives in Klyuchevoi or Chulesh village. This shaman prefers not to talk about herself and so few of her fellow villagers know her life's story. We received different versions in answer to our questions concerning her life. For example, when we first asked her to describe her

Photo: Alexander Arbachakov

Evdokiya Gavrilovna Todyyakova

family she said that she had one son. The second time she was asked she said that she had several children and the third time she was asked Evdokiya Gavrilovna replied that she had no family. It is extremely difficult to catch her at home as she rarely actually stays there. In the summer she helps her fellow villagers rake in the hay and then in the winter she stays with friends due to the fact that her house is rickety and cold.

E. G. Todyyakova began practising shamanism when she was fifteen years old having received the gift from the son of her Great-grandmother who was shot in the 1920's-30's by the Cossacks who discovered a drum in his home. She told us: "The son of my Great-grandmother on my father's side was a great shaman. He had a drum and rattle and when the Russians shot him in Solton (village in Tashtagol'skii region) his spirits came to me."

She expressed her sorrow that no great shamans are left today. Before, the people assisted the shaman in making his drum. They killed a roe-deer for the drum's handle. A birch branch was bent into an arc and 'kuiak' (protective attributes) were hung from it. Here they called the ancestral spirits. "Ulug kamnar olpargannar". The great kam have passed away. "Pozu ishter kerek." The people must continue to live and work. "Turu sabynga kiiik adarga kerek." An animal must be killed for food. "Aga kuiktar ishtechen." The birch should be bent into an arc. "Kam adalyryn adalcha, tostin ady." The kam speaks the names of her male ancestors.

Evdokiya Gavrilovna
Todyyakova

Photo: Llyn Roberts

E. G. Todyyakova was visited for the first time in the summer of 1998 by L.N. Arbachakova and the ethno-musicologist R.B. Nazarenko. Initially Evdokiya Gavrilovna was wary of her guests as she was rarely approached by non Shor individuals with the request to conduct kamlanie. On the request of these researchers Evdokiya Gavrilovna performed 'Eski Churt' and then she conducted a healing kamlanie on behalf of R.B. Nazarenko who was feeling unwell.

The next visit to Evdokiya Gavrilovna by the authors took place in 1999. On this occasion she was evidently more comfortable in receiving guests, even allowing them to photograph her on completion of the ritual. On our request she performed 'Eski Churt' (kamlanie to ancestral spirits) again. She used a towel during the ritual, explaining that someone had thrown out her 'shorbu' (birch branch).

We visited Evdokiya Gavrilovna last in November 1999. This time she conducted a 'House Cleansing' ritual to drive out any dark spirits. After the ceremony she said that the author's nephew, Ilya, had fallen ill because his Ymai (in her words - the child's soul) had fallen down and died. She then said that all would now be well because she had managed to raise Ilya's Ymai.

Of her spirit helpers she said: My spirits tread the clouds whereas I walk the road. "Men tosterim pulutpa parchar, men cholba parcham."

During kamlanie she addresses the mountains Mustag, Kubes, Kol taiga and Sanash tag. Her path is blessed by Ot eezi algapcha (fire spirit). She believes the Fire spirit to be extremely powerful and able to draw out worms and lizards (i.e. the dark spirits of the Underworld) which she then destroys. "Otka shoktebiskem. Ottar to chylannar, to kileskenner shykchar. Ot eezi kushtig, shube tartchi. Ol shoshkannardy, kileskennerdi tartchi. Men ylardy odurubuskem."

When asked about the clan mountain Mustag, she said: All the kam go there with offerings but I go without offerings. At Mustag they wait for me and ask me, "Why don't you make us offerings of the home-brew?" (Tiken aara kait perbedin? – tepchalar)

Evdokiya Gavrilovna conducts kamlanie at her house in Klyucheva. Before starting she poured a glass of vodka (often used as a substitute for spirit drink in offerings), sipped a little, placed a spoon beside the glass and then began the kamlanie. She sat on a stool, rhythmically waving a birch branch, 'shorbu'. At one point during the kamlanie she got up and walked over to the stove to make an offering to the Fire spirit. She sprinkled vodka with the spoon three times and then returned to her stool and continued with the ritual.

Todyyakova begins kamlanie with 'shachyg', (libation): Shog – shogoi. She gathers her spirit helpers with the help of a 'hard tula' – 'kazyr tula'. (According to the reminiscences of Shor elders a tula is similar to a drum handle piece to which pieces of squirrel or chipmunk skin are attached.) The spirits come from under the earth from the Samchyk rocks and uncle Kamchyk. Having gathered her spirit helpers about her the kam then addresses 'Ul'gen': Pajhyn ulgen, pai Ul'gen', Great Ul'gen, pai* Ul'gen.

At the beginning of the kamlanie the kam must symbolically

leave the real world and enter the spirit world. To do so she must cross (overcome) the sacred (light, white) boundary - 'Ak shedennin ashkyiakym', (I have not yet crossed the Sacred boundary).

Opening (overcoming) and entering the sacred, white boundary is an essential stage at the beginning of the kamlanie. According to our informant L.N. Arbachakova the white boundary is a light, pure road. The black boundary in its turn is the dark road. If a person comes to a kam with pure thoughts then the kam takes the light road whereas if a person comes with dark thoughts the kam takes the dark road. (Kara sheden kara choluba parchyn sheden. Kara sagyshtyg kijhege kara cholba, kara sheden ash-kel, parcha. Ak sagyshtyg kijhi polganda, ak cholba, ak shedeni ashcha.)

Having crossed the boundary the kam can proceed further. Approaching 'Eski churt', Todyyakova sprinkles the most well-known places which are the upper reaches of the sacred Pyzas river and the peak of Anzass Mountain. Then, pronouncing her father's surname she said that she was conducting the ritual for 'the one with skirt', meaning 'for a woman'. (Evdokiya Gavrilovna made a mistake in pronouncing the father's surname as Bashev when it should have been Tudegeshev. She may have heard the surname incorrectly or perhaps have temporarily forgotten it during the kamlanie.)

In Todyyakova's kamlanie she addresses the magnificent sacred birch tree. As has been mentioned previously, in the Shor worldview the birch symbolises the world tree that joins the three worlds. The birch accompanies a person throughout their whole life in different forms. Birch branches are tied to a girl's cradle as a symbol of her future marriage. Cradles were even made from birch wood. The 'shalash', 'cabin' constructed for the newly weds at their wedding was made from birch branch and all kitchen utensils were made from birch. During kamlanie a bunch of small birch branches called 'shorbu' may be used in place of the drum. As noted before, the kam communicates with the Higher Deities by climbing the birch tree.

Parak pashtyg pai kazynash,	Magnificent, sacred birch,
Pai Ulgenin kyiyk polbas,	Pai'* Ul'gen will place no prohibition/inter-diction
okcha shabarga ochanarym.	To shoot the arrow I commit myself.
otka shabarga orgenarym.	To shoot the fire I shall learn.

In our opinion E.G. Todyyakova's text of the kamlanie 'Eski Churt' is the most archaic. It contains many mythical images and motifs such as the Samchyk rocks, sacred boundary, copper fly, copper breast, Khan Ojhakai, six and seven-eyed horsefly, Cheles (invisible) fly and uncle Kamchyk. Aside from the mythical figures in the text real names and geographical place names are included such as the sacred Pyzass River which flows not far from Anzass village. Todyyakova also makes reference to the village of Anzass itself and performs libation to the Anzass peaks.

At the end of a kamlanie the shaman always gives a yawn. The Khakass kam say that in this way they gather back their spirit-helpers. The Shor kam K. Chudekov did the opposite, yawning before the kamlanie which suggests that he gathers his spirit helpers externally to himself whereas Todyyakova releases her spirits and then retrieves them.

* 'Pai' – has no direct translation into English. It means, 'rich', 'sacred', or 'prohibition' 'Ban' in the sense that certain prohibitions and behavioural codes are observed to protect the essence of that which is sacred.

Kirill Prokop'evich Chudekov

Kirill Prokop'evich Chudekov (1921-2001) was born in Purla village in the Tashtagolskii rayon. He worked for many years as Chairman of the Kholkoz in the outskirts of Spassk and then later in Tashtagol, where he lived until the end of his life.

Kirill Prokop'evich held to an incredible combination paganism and Orthodoxy and illustrates the result of Christianization on the traditional Shor worldview. He says himself that he always goes to church and prays in the mornings but that doesn't stop him from conducting kamlanie.

He began practising shamanism when he was fifteen years old although there previously were no shamans in his clan. Chudekov suffered with the shaman's illness for a long time until people explained to him that the reason for the illness was that he was being tormented by a kams' spirits. From that time onwards he began conducting kamlanie. Kirill Prokop'evich believes that a kam has to suffer for a long time. 'Without illness, there can be no kam'.

Kirill Prokop'evich practises without the use of a drum because 'there are no drum masters left now'. (Buben ishtep perchin kijhi am chok.) In his opinion the drum should be made by elderly individuals from the skin of a taiga animal. The kam does not have the right to make the drum himself. Of his spirit helpers Kirill Prokop'rvich said that he has two. 'I ask them for advice and then speak what I have been told. They guide me in what to do next.' (Ylardyn surap-kel, aitcham, ylar noo ishterge aitchar)

The kam said that his spirit-helpers look similar to people and speak in the Shor language. They help him in the battle against evil spirits and clear the 'road' so that it is open. (Cholum ashyk polzyn.)

Chudekov told us that when he meets other kam's spirits he tries to avoid them and not disturb them unnecessarily. 'There is one shamaness I know. It happens that we meet but I leave her alone. I can recognise her by her smell. I see her. She's old now." Of Tashtagol'skii Mustag Mountain the kam said that the mountain was large and had a huge amount of energy; that there were many dark spirits there. He believes that the mountain che ezi and spirits have ears which open up in the spring, i.e. they begin to hear in the spring. (Tag eezinin ai kulagy ashyl-pardy chaskyda) In the autumn their ears close and they hear nothing

again until the following spring. (Kushudi ai kulagy tun-parcha)
As a result, the kam also hear more in the spring. (Kamnyn
chaskyda kulagy chaksharak ukchalar) Kam hear what is
happening in the other worlds with their 'moon ears' and then re-
tell what they have heard to those present. (Ai kulak uluglupkel
aitchalar)

We recorded Kirill Prokop'evich for the first time in 1998 (see
verses section). At our request he performed the 'Eski Churt'
ritual. The second recording of Chudekov's 'Eski Churt' (ancestor
kamlanie) was made in June 2001. During the kamlanie Kirill
Prokop'evich used a towel, a headscarf, the scarf of the person
fallen ill, vodka and money. This ritual was conducted at L.
Arbachakova's request. Before beginning the kamlanie the kam
asked her about her parents and where she lived. When told that
her parents lived in Anzass village he replied that he had been to
that area and so would have no difficulties in journeying there.

Kirill Prokop'evich asks visitors who have come for help to
cover their head and not to remove their shoes. In his opinion
dark spirits cannot fall on his trail if the visitor is dressed in hat
and shoes.

The kam then sat on a stool, picked up the towel and began his
kamlanie. At one point during the ritual he went up to the stove
and conducted the 'shachyg' offering to the fire spirit. He also
approached L. Arbachakova and passed the towel three times
around her head, shaking it constantly.

Chudekov began the kamlanie with interjections of "O-o!", but
he took a long time in preparing himself for the kamlanie proper
and often coughed between words. Evidently to distract or
deceive the spirits he would begin a conversation about the
weather: 'Strange that there is no rain. It's dry here. I don't
suppose the potatoes are growing.' He asked about the weather a
second time and only then began the full kamlanie:

O-o, chaiky chidemnin shiiil sal turokbanym,
O-o, I shall rise up and slap the swinging reins,

Kamchi pajhy shokul turzunan,
May the crack of the kam's lash be heard,
Aksy-tilemnin kiberti alaibanym,
Mouth-tongue rituals-traditions I obtain.

According to the reminiscence of the elderly, if a kam had no drum he would use a lash instead. Evil spirits however, were only driven out of the house with a whip. The image of the lash which fulfils a cleansing function is repeated by the kam throughout the whole text as an incantation:

Kamchy-pajhy shiiil turzyn.
May the tip of the lash wave – draw.

Pargan cholum ashyk polzun, o-o!
May the road ahead be open o-o!

Olen pajhy nugur turzyn, o-o!
May the tips of the grass sway past, o-o!

Agash pajhy nugur turzun, o-o!
May the tops of the trees sway past, o-o!

This image varies in the following lines:

Kyrchyn pajhy topchulug polchyn, kaia!
May 'kyrchyn' grow soft and rounded!

Kamchy pajhy sheshtig polchyn, kaia!
May the end of the lash be untied!

Shaktyn pajhy chyltyryg polchun, kaia!
May the game bones shine!

Setting off on his journey the kam pronounces the surname of the house owner: "O-o, I disturb the Tudegeshev churt."

Approaching the 'Deserted Churt' he finds the ancestor's grave and asks of the possible outcome of the healing. "May it be as you decide." Learning of the ancestor's decision the kam then calms them. "May clasped hands fall to the side. May the worried heart be calmed."

Then he returns by the same road as he set out. Returning to the world of day the kam constantly pronounces words associated with healing substances: "I carry a healing light with me." This is evidently necessary for protection from dark spirits. On the journey the kam makes a symbolic sacrifice of a foal: "When I cross the seven rivers I shall sacrifice a foal."

Chudekov calls his spirit-helpers Ugalchy, which means 'listeners'. He refers to a woman allegorically as: "in the hands of the one with skirt, it seems, o-o!"

Anis'ya Afanas'evna Tudegesheva

Anis'ya Afanas'evna Tudegesheva (1922-1999) was born in Kolzass village (Chilissu-Anzasskii village soviet) and moved to El'beza village when she married.

As far as she can remember, there had always been shamans in her clan. The spirits had passed her mother by and chosen her. Tudegesheva recounts that when the spirits fell on her trail searching for a 'extra bone' she suffered for a long time even to the point of wanting to commit suicide. She says, "Whatever you do, don't become a kam!" (Toos kelgende, mongen, erelengen: 'Kam polarga Kudai perbezin!') She finally began practising kamlanie when she was advised to do so by her aunt and other individuals.

The only sound recording made of Tudegesheva performing 'Eski Churt' was made in 1998. The kam knew L. Arbachakova's parents and home village and so she did not hesitate in agreeing to conduct the ritual.

A.A. Tudegesheva performed the kamlanie sitting on a small stool. She began with interjectory incantations of 'A-Ek!' She held a heavy glove filled with sand or clay which she waved monotonously throughout the kamlanie.

Tudegesheva calls her spirit-helpers 'managers or bosses who

must learn the decisions of my relatives.'
The kam reaches the 'Deserted Churt' saying:

A-ek, now Anzass,
E-eh, I will walk through her.

Like Kirill Chudekov, Anis'ya Afanas'evna also mentions the
sacrifice of a stallion during the ritual: 'The stallion needs to be
slaughtered.' She also makes offerings to the spirits calling them
by mythical names:

A-eh, here is Tabiltir.
A-eh, give some to kypchaki.

At the end of the kamlanie Tudegesheva figuratively dresses
herself in armour in a curious form of protection.

A-eh, I wear nine coats of mail.
A-eh, I am robed in seven coats of mail.

An analysis of the text shows that it consists of three main parts:

Calling the spirit-helpers
Journeying to the 'deserted churt'
Return to the world of day

Vasilii Savel'evich Ady'yakov

Vasilii Savel'evich Ady'yakov (1919-1995) was born in Naachal
village (Kabyrzinskii village soviet) where he lived all his life. He
worked in the kolkhoz and then later as a hunter, game-shooter.
He served in the war where he suffered wounds.

Unfortunately, we were only able to meet him on one occasion
in 1994. At that time he was ill and said that he was unable to
battle with powerful spirits and so we asked him to conduct a
ritual called 'The Soul Catch'. (The text of this kamlanie was
included in the manuscript of the volume entitled 'Fol'klor

Vasilii Savel'evich Ady'yakov

Shortsev') At first he performed a rough version of the kamlanie and so we did not record him. Thinking that his guests did not speak Shor he turned to his daughter and said that he had performed the ritual jokingly. We then asked him to perform the ritual again but this time in all seriousness.

Vasilii Savel'evich Ady'yakov told us about his spirit-helpers who he called 'karolchuktar' or 'toster': "I draw my spirits from the mountains. There are a lot of spirits in the rivers also. There are spirit-helpers in the sky and under the ground even. A good kam has kind spirits. When my spirits have overcome an evil spirit they turn it into a snake which goes to attack me. I then chop them up with my lash." (Snakes are figuratively referred to as 'uzun kuzuruk' – 'the long tailed')

The kamlanie began with an address to Ul'gen who the kam calls 'Ul'gen khan': 'O-oi, Ulgen khaanym, kaan polarzyn.' (Oh, my khan Ulgen, be khan.) The God Ul'gen is supposed to give his final decision regarding the lost soul. The kam addresses his spirit-helpers 'oolkystarym', (literally meaning 'my boys and girls'). He gathers his spirit-helpers from Mother-fire and having collected them up he sets out with them in search of the lost soul. They look in the rivers, among the fish, in the mountains and even search the earth from the skies. Finally, when the kam has found the soul he blows it into the patient through their ears.

The kamlanie as a whole consists of an invocation to the spirits, the search for the lost soul, and once it has been located, its return to the patient.

V.S. Ady'yakov conducted the 'soul catch' ritual sitting on a stool and waving a towel. At the end of the kamlanie when he had found the soul he stood up in order to blow it into the patient's ears.

Kristina Nikolaevna Ady'yakova

Kristina Nikolaevna Ady'yakova was born in 1930 in Matur

village (no longer existing). Now she lives in Naachol village (Kabyrzinskii village soviet). During her working life Kristina Nikolaevna worked in the 'Naa Chol' 'New Way' kolkhoz and is now a pensioner.

Ady'yakova told us that she first began practising shamanism relatively recently in 1994. Before then she had 'heard 'shaitan' (Saitan) for eleven years, suffered from amnesia, run away from home and spoken with the spirits of Karatag mountain (situated in the vicinity of Ust'Kabypza village)...'

Kristina Nikolaevna believes that the mountain spirits are at Mustag in the winter returning to Karatag in April. Her spirits never sleep, are similar to people in outward appearance, although somewhat smaller and speak in Shor.

Kristina Nikolaevna was well acquainted with her kam neighbour V.S. Ady'yakov and told us that he began practising shamanism in the 1970's but before that had practised 'pulse-divination', 'kol tutkan'. When he was about fifty years old he began to suffer from the 'shaman's illness' after which he became a practising shaman. Unlike Kristina Nikolaevna his parents were powerful shamans.

Kristina Nikolaevna Ady'yakova conducted the ritual kamlanie 'Home Cleansing' which was recorded in January 1995. The text of the recording was also included in the manuscript of the volume 'Fol'klor Shortsev'. She sat on a stool facing the door to do the ritual waving a towel in poetic rhythm. Before starting she joked turning to one of the authors saying: 'I'll take you along with me, ok?'

In addition to the realistic element such as the mention of Karatag mountain situated in the vicinity of Naachol, the kam also used figurative and magical words of which she did not always know the meanings herself.

The text of the kamlanie can be roughly divided into three parts:

Invoking the spirits which the shaman called 'my shadows':

O-oi, my shadows,
E-ek, the clear blue,
E-ek, we shall try to intervene.

Observation of the place:

A-ei, look,
E-ei, father-kurum.
E-ei, look.
E-ei from the blue 'taskil'*
......passing by the taskil

Return of the spirits for the purposes of protection:

E-ei, don't leave yet, stay, I robe.
E-ei, in your churt,
Ei, when they return,
E-ei when they do not understand, I shall robe them.

After the kamlanie Kristina Nikolaevna told the woman for whom she had conducted the ritual: 'Some-one who is jealous of you wishes you harm. They have placed certain objects in your garden and vegetable patch.' Then she reassured her saying: 'All will be well now.'

*Taskil – is a high view point in the taiga. From a taskil the view which is normally obscured by trees and undergrowth is clear all around. The 'taskil' is described as blue no doubt because the landscape takes on a blue hue either from the reflection of light from the sky or snow.

Marfa Fedorovna Kiskorova
Marfa Fedorovna claims that she is not a shaman but an 'alaschi kijhi' which is a person who gives blessing and works as a healer: "I only do healing work. My father was a kam and something of him has been passed on to me." At the time we visited Marfa

Fedorovna she had been practising for three years.

Before the ritual kamlanie, 'Healing the Sick', Kiskorova asked the patient to give her their kerchief and some vodka. The 'alaschi kijhi' (blesser/healer) poured the vodka for us and for herself. We declined and Kiskorova drank a small, liquor glass full. Then she took the patient's hat (instead of the kerchief) and began the ritual. She sat the patient on a stool and began passing the hat up and down her body for cleansing and to drive the dark spirits away and spoke the words 'alamna, alamna'.

Short breaks for rest were made during the kamlanie as Kiskorova was herself unwell at that time and so tired easily.

An analysis of the interpreted text reveals that the content of the lines does not always have recognizable meaning. In terms of composition the different parts of the text are linked by a single theme. This text can also be roughly divided into three parts.

In the first part the shaman tries to determine the cause of the ill or illness that has seized the patient. With this goal in mind the 'aalaschi' begins the ritual by examining the patient's spine and trying to determine where the ill is located in the body, meanwhile addressing God and Maria.

U-u, have you come from the mountains or from the sleepy forest?

I-I, does the ill come from man or the earth?

O-o, My god, on high,
O-o, Maria, on high.

In the second part Marfa Fedorovna invokes her spirit-helpers so that they may examine the patient:

Go and look at her ancestors.
Fy-fy, do not take the one who has skirt with you.
Have you studied the one who has skirt?
During the kamlanie she acquaints herself with the patient also:

'O-o, speak your name, speak your name!'
She asks: 'What is her name?'
We reply: 'Karmen!'

The process ends with Marfa driving out the illness and evil spirits from the body:

'O-o, free yourself from the body, leave the body.
Free yourself from the body, leave the body.'

At this point she runs the headscarf along Karmen's (the patient) body and shakes out the scarf.

Akulina Osipovna Kuspekova

We made several recordings of Akulina Osipovna Kuspekova. 'The Deserted Churt' was recorded in August 2000; 'The Deceased' was recorded in June 2001 and 'Alas Lyube' in August 2003. The sound recording from 2000 was also included in the volume 'Kol'klor Shortsev'.

Akulina Osipovna Kuspekova was born in Seizak village in 1930. Up until her pensioner's years she lived and worked in Tashtagol town. Once retiring for her well-earned rest Akulina Osipovna purchased a small home in Aleksandrovka village where she now lives with her husband.

Like all kam Akulina Osipovna suffered severely from the 'shaman's illness' and then began practising shamanism in 1999. The spirits, 'toster' told her: 'Either you will die or you will become a kam.' Kuspekova remembers that her mother Ekaterina Cozygasheva, born in Karagol, must have been a powerful shaman because she used a drum during kamlanie. After her mother's death the spirits came to Akulina. She has also received spirit-helpers from relatives of the Achulakovii clan.

When conducting a ritual kamlanie Kuspekova uses a 'shorbu' (bundle of small birch branches) and changes into a white (doctors) coat. She also always covered her head with a light coloured head scarf. This is necessary she believes 'for the spirits to be able to identify the person's trail.' The kam then places a glass of vodka in front of her and conducts libation during the kamlanie making offerings to the spirits.

On analysis of the text it became evident that Kuspekova gathered her spirit-helpers using a lash:

A-ei, those who are with the one I look to understand, gather together.

A-ok, the time has come for my soul to twist.

A-ei, I call my spirits.

A-ei, I call them with the sound of my lash.

The kam sees her spirit-helpers in the form of thirty-nine horses which she drives with her lash:

'A-a, adamnyn odus togus 'A-a, my father's thirty-nine horses,

At plarbus, kamchylaiym! I call you with my lash!' (translator's addition)

Here Kuspekova berates herself and asks the spirits to forgive her for having burned her 'shorbu' (birch bundle) in the fire. Previously to the kamlanie she told us that she had been celebrating and couldn't remember how she had burned the shorbu:

'A-ek, you threw your sacred shorbu on the fire, foolish woman.'

During the kamlanie however, no mention would be made of this fact, neither would she berate herself for it.

In the second part she asks the name of the person the kamlanie is being conducted for (in this case 'Lyuba' – L.N. Arbacchakova); gathers the spirits; studies the place where the person lives; makes offerings to the spirits and learns of their decision. At the end of the kamlanie she mentally 'girds'* all those present with 'armour' (a protective aura).

All the ritual kamlanie of 'Eski Churt' can be roughly divided into three parts:

The beginning of the journey to 'Eski Churt'. The kam sets off on her journey with her spirit-helpers and the help of incantations for example, to the churt of the Tudegeshev family.

Achieving the goal. The kam and her spirit-helpers reach the Tudegeshev churt and communicate with the ancestral spirits, learning of their decision.

Returning to the starting point. Having learned of the ancestor's decision, the spirit helpers and she returns together with them. Before leaving, she calms the disturbed spirits and carries out libation at their resting place.

Generally speaking, although the two kamlanie described in this book have their own magical content and meaning, they all conform to the same three part structure.

* 'Girds' / 'girdles' or 'belting' is a ritual action involving winding a piece of material or a belt or energy around a person's waist to protect their naval area.

KAMLANIE VERSES OF TWO KAM

The texts of shamanic verse – two versions of the shamanic kamlanie 'Eski Churt' – are published here in English for the first time. Sound recordings for both kamlanie verses are executed by L.N. Arbachakov.

Photo: Llyn Roberts

KAMLANIE ONE: "The Deserted Churt"
Shaman Kirill Prokop'evich Chudekov

Bridge in Shor Territory

1. O-o, I will rise up, and slap the swinging reins* (note a.
   below),
May the tip of my lash* (note b. below) plunge.
I will find the mouth-tongue customs-traditions,
O-o, I shall try to rock the shoulder and head.* (note c. below)
U-u, if the swinging reins are shaken,
I will shake them and strike through now,
Finding the mouth-tongue, customs-traditions
I shall put my right ear to listening,
May they open the board-door.

10. Take the mouth-tongue customs-traditions, O-o!
O-o, I incline my right ear o-o.
You will see, Eze!
I shall try and shake the shoulders and head.
May the end of my lash wave and draw.
May the road I travel be open, o-o!

May the tops of the grasses sway past, o-o!
May the crowns of the trees bow down, o-o!
(This) you will see, Eze!
To loosen the shoulders and head I try,

20. May the tips of the grasses unfold,
May the crowns of the trees bow down.
(This) you will see, Eze!
O-o, I make to visit the Tudegeshev churt.[1]
And you will hear what they have to say,
Which laws this churt lives by, (to which higher court they
    swear).
May they see (this), Eze!
I incline my right ear.
May the road ahead be open.

30. May the tops of the grasses sway past.
May the crowns of the trees bow down, o-o!
May the eze see (this), o-o.
May the head of 'kyrchyn'* (note d. below) be rounded,
May the end of the lash be untied,
May the head of the game bones shine, * (note e. below)
(This) you will see!
I incline my moon ears, o-o![2]
To which court will be it be submitted, o-o!
If the free doors swing wide,

40. They beat, o-o!
If the land really does have defence (armour),
They will stand secure and firm,
Let this be seen, eze!
The supporting pole (note f. below) of the house I secure,
When the court is uncertain, undecided,
When the shoulders and head try to shake,
I will observe the mouth-tongue, customs-traditions,
May your judgment-decision come to pass.[3]

When the shoulders-head shake

50. May the decision of the court be open, o-o!
As I walked I had healing substance,[4]
When I arrived I had magic incantation.
Let them see (this), eze!
If your judgment is considered,
We will understand it; do not change from side to side,
Closing the decision, declare (it).
We will see
The judgment which has been passed, o-o!
And the court that has made the final decision!

60. If you approach the spirit-helpers, I will hold a court, o-o!
Let them resurrect the mouth-tongue customs-traditions.
May they open the board-door.
They will see the shoulders-head that shake, o-o!
Let them see (this), eze!
May they hear your judgment.
I incline my moon ears, o-o!
I will be in time to squeeze through the doors of the earth, o-o!
May the path I journey be pure, o-o!
I follow the mouth-tongue, customs-traditions.

70. I incline my moon ears.
Let them open your door with the six handle-locks.
For when I arrived it was with magical incantation.
The incantations appeared when I reach the end, o-o!
I stood with half the armour,
When half the armour appeared,
The path I took was opened it seems,
I walk the earth, and light my way,
I force my way through the taiga,
In the land I visit may they too
make their way through the taiga,
In which side are we, what a harsh, scorching lash,

80. For the end of the lash was untied.
What court will they create?
Your doors to the land stand open,
For when I came, I came with incantation,
When I arrived, it was with healing substances,
O-o, I am half way there.
I incline my moon ears, what court will you gather?
O-o, I have crossed seven passes,
Seven rivers I shall wade across, and then a colt I shall
    sacrifice.[5]

90. Seven skies I shall pass, then I shall arrive,
May they see this, eze!
May the doors with rusty handle-locks open.
For when I go, I go with healing substances,
For when I arrive it is by incantation.
Let them see, eze!
I sacrificed a colt.
O-o, when my half armoured coat swings open,
When the doors of your land are open,
Then we shall see, eze!

100. What payment will they take?
We will stand guessing, (comparing-considering).
I find the mouth-tongue customs-traditions.
I will try and share half the place.
If the door to your land hangs off and sways,
What judgment will your lying body pass on us?[6]
The seven defences, (armour) which you counted on,
could not compare with my power.
Shaking the shoulders-head I go.
I find the mouth-tongue customs-traditions.

110. What judgment will you pass?
All is in the hands of the one with skirt.
Move up to her,

Take your measure from her, eze!
O-o, I do not know; may they consider all.
They are in meaning of equal standing,
In the midnight darkness judgment will be passed.
Let them see (this), eze!
O-o, a-a, the judgment of the court is nearing.
They stood and compared, o-o!
When the court's judgment is applied

120. Let them stand and compare (then).
The judgment will be passed on the seventh night.
Let them see (this), eze!
I implemented that trial (initiation),
They counted on half the armour,
Because the doors to the land were closed,
Because the land's defence (armour) turned out to be light,
That judgment I implemented.
May they watch, eze!
Whatever payment you demand,
I make to bless her![7]

130. Do not wander from side to side,
(then) you will receive my offering (libation).
You have made it equal to the thirty-headed fire mother,
I will make the mourning head of sorrowful flame[8]
Equal to white water.
Let them see, eze!
When the doors to the land open,
(then) we will stand and compare.
May my land narrow.
Do not waver from side to side.
Drink my offerings, o-o!

140. Here things happen in a special way.
My land is nearing,
You will sense its smell.

(Khrap) Inhale the smells of division
While the door to the land is open,
While the shields of the land truly rise (before us),
Value (them), o-o!
Take measure from the thirty-headed fire mother,
Why are there no four shields to the land?
The four corners are so dark,

150. The guest imposed a punishment on them.
This we will see!
That is the court's decision I have implemented.
When the defence of the land truly rises, o-o,
I shall leave the land
of the thirty-headed fire mother, o-o!
May it measure to the judgment (of the court).
You will see, eze!
May the heads of friends not rock
O-o he was probably captured.

160. May clasped hands fall to the side
And the anxious heart be quieted.
May the land not shake from side to side.
May they pull her so that she stands level.
May the thirty-headed fire mother
 impose no punishment, shok!
That is the decision I implemented,
        that is how I judged it.
May the incantation hold sure, not wander here and there,
Let them watch, eze!
Don't put up the seven boundaries,

170. Impose no punishment, change places,
Don't look around, up or down,
        (neither look at yourself)
I stand and compare (evaluate), shog!
When I implemented the judgment,

Cause no humiliation,
For there is metal at the end of the lash,
I will hold the balance, o-o!
For order will remain unbroken,
Don't turn back or look around,
Change places.

180. That is the decision I implemented,
May they accept our payment kindly,
So that this healing substance take effect,
Change places.
Don't turn around and watch.
Not acknowledging the mouth-tongue customs-traditions,
Not inclining the moon ears,
Change places, sheg!
That is the judgment of the court I administered,
O-o, when the door to the land stood and beat,
It came to pass, ku-ku!

190. I shall try to return
I shall drive the many-coloured horses.
What was opened will close,
     it can be heard.
I shall try to return, listener,
Nine belts, listener,
Tied in a knot, listener, ku-ku!
I shall try to return.

200. I will try to change place.
Here and there, listener, do not wander
Listener, make more offerings (libation), ku-ku!
O-o, I shall rise, slap the swinging reins,
May the end of my lash plunge.
I find the mouth-tongue customs-traditions,
O-o I will try not to shake the shoulders-head.
U-u, if the swaying reins flap,

I will slap them now.
Finding the mouth-tongue customs-traditions,
I incline my tight ear to listen.
May they open the board-door.

210. Receive the mouth-tongue customs-traditions, o-o!
O-o, I incline my right ear o-o,
You will see (this), eze!
I will try to shake the shoulders-head,
May the end of my lash lunge.
May the road I walk be open, o-o!
May the tips of the grasses sway, o-o!
May the tops of the trees twist, o-o!

220. Let them watch, eze!
I tried to rock the shoulders-head,
May the tops of the grasses bloom,
May the tops of the trees, twist.
May they watch, eze!
O-o, I make to visit the Tudegeshev churt.
And you will hear of what they speak,
And you will hear what they speak,
Which laws this churt lives by, (to which higher court they
    swear).
May they see (this), Eze!
I incline my right ear.

230. May the road I walk be open.
Do not wander from side to side.
May the tips of the grasses sway,
May the tops of the trees bow down, o-o!
May they see (this), eze, o-o.
May the head of 'kyrchyn' be rounded,
May the end of the lash be untied,
May the head of the bone shine,

(This) you will see!
My moon ears incline, o-o!

240. What judgment will be passed, o-o!
If the free doors swing
They strike, sound, o-o!
If the land truly had defence (armour),
They would stand firm and secure.
Let them see (this), eze!
I secure the support-pole of the home
When the court is uncertain, divided,
When the shoulders-head rock,
I try to follow the mouth-tongue customs-traditions.

250. May your judgment pass.
When the shoulder-head rocks,
May the decision of the court be open, o-o!
For when I went I had healing substance,
When I arrived it was with magical incantation.
Let them see (this), eze.
If your judgment is well considered,
Declare it, we will see (it),
Do not swing from side to side,
Passing (the decision), declare (it).

260. Your judgment has been passed
The court has made a final decision, o-o!
We will see!
When you approach the spirit-helpers,
I will implement the judgment, o-o!
May they establish the mouth-tongue customs-traditions.
May they open the board-door,
The shoulders-head will begin to move, o-o!
Let them see, eze!
May they think on the verdict.
I incline my moon ears, o-o!

I will slip through the land's door in time, o-o!

270. May the road by which I go be open. o-o!
I find the mouth-tongue, customs-traditions.
Inclining my moon ears, I stand.
May the doors with six handles open.
When I arrive it is with incantation,
The incantations appeared when I reach the end, o-o!
Having taken half the armour, I stood,
When the half armour appeared
The road by which I travelled was open, it seemed.
I walk the land, light my way,
I force my way through the taiga,

280. In the land I visit may they too
make their way through the taiga,
In which side are we, what a harsh, scorching lash,
For the end of the lash was untied.
What judgment will they make?
Because the doors to your land stand open,
When I came, I came with incantation,
When I arrived I arrived with healing substances it appears.
O-o, I have travelled half the journey.
My moon eras I incline,
What judgment will you make?

290. O-o, seven mountain passes I shall pass,
Seven rivers I have waded across,
A colt I shall sacrifice.
Seven skies I shall pass before I arrive,
Let them watch (this), eze!
May the doors with rusty handles-locks open.
When I go it is with healing substance,
When I arrive it will be with incantation.
Let them watch, eze!
I sacrificed a colt.

300. O-o, when the half armour opened,
When the door to the land opened,
He will see, eze!
What payment will they take?
We will stand and guess (comparing-counting)
The mouth-tongue customs-traditions I find.
We will try to share half the place with each other.
If the door to your land hangs and sways
What judgment can your lying body pass on us?
The seven defences (armour) that you counted on

310. Could not compare with my strength.
Shoulders-head rocking I go.
I find the mouth-tongue customs-traditions.
What judgment will you pass on me?
(All is) in the hands of she with skirt, it seems.
Approach her,
Takes one's measure from her, eze!
O-o, I do not know, let them take measure.
Those equal in standing (in meaning) have implemented
    punishment, it seems.
Let them see (this), eze!

320. O-o, a-a, the judgment of the court is nearing,
They stood and compared, o-o!
When such a judgment is implemented,
May they stand and compare.
The judgment will come on the seventh night.
Watch eze!
That is the trial I have implemented.
He counted on half the armour, eze.
Because the doors to the land were closed,
Because the defence (armour) of the land turned out to be
    light.

330. That is the judgment I have implemented.

Let them watch, eze!
Whatever payment you take,
I make to bless her!
Do not sway from side to side
    then you will accept my offering (libation).
You have put it equal with the thirty-headed fire mother.
I put the mourning head of sorrowful flame
equal to white water.
Let them see, eze!
When the door of the land opens,

340. We will stand and compare,
May my land narrow.
Do not sway from side to side.
Drink my offering!
Here things can happen in a special way.
My land is nearing,
You will sense her smell.
Inhale the smell of division.
While the door of the land is open,
While the shields (armour) of the land truly rise (before us),

350. Enjoy (them), o-o!
Take measure from the thirty-headed fire mother.
Why are there no four shields to the land?
The four corners are so dark,
The guest imposed punishment.
This we will see!
That is the judgment made.
That is the judgment, o-o!
When the earth's armour rang, o-o!
I will give place to the thirty-headed fire mother, o-o!

360. May they listen to the judgment.
Let the watch, eze,
(May) The heads of friends not rock, o-o!

They have probably been captured.
(May) they let go their clasped hands,
May the worried heart cool.
May the land not sway from side to side.
May they pull you up, I take measure.
May no punishment be imposed,
By the thirty-headed fire mother shek!

370. This is the decision I have made, compared.
Evaluating I stood.
The incantation which I made,
Has not ended (not closed) since that time.
Let them watch!
Do not put up the seven (boundaries),
Impose no punishment, change places.
Don't look around, back or down,
I stand, compare (evaluate), shog!
When such a judgment I implement.

380. Make no kind of punishment,
For the end of the lash may have a clump.
I will place her equal, o-o!
For order will be undisturbed,
Do not look back or turn around.
Change places.
That is the decision I made.
May they take
our payment kindly.
So that this healing substance take effect,

390. Change places.
Don't look round, don't watch.
Not perceiving the mouth-tongue customs-traditions,
Moon ears not inclining,
Change places, sheg!
That is the judgment I implemented.

O-o, When the door to the land began to stand and beat,
It was manifested, ku-ku!
I will try and return,
I shall drive the many-coloured horses.

400. You can hear that what was pulled out is closing.
I shall try and return, listener, ku-ku!
The door of the land, listener,
Are arrows being fired?
The end of the lash, listener,
Is sometimes tied in a knot, listener, ku-ku!
I will try and return,
I will try and change places.
Don't wander hither and thither, listener.

410. Listener, make offerings of libation again, ku-ku!
Ku-ky, o-o!

Notes to the Shamanic Verse

No. 1 "Eski Churt"
(Kam Chudekov K.P., sound recording, interpretation and original translation from Shor to Russian by L.N. Arbachakova)

1. 'O-o, I make to visit the Tudegeshev churt' - this is the surname of the previous owners of the churt.

2. 'I incline my moon ears' - According to the kam and other Shor elders the mountain che ezi and other spirits have moon ears which open up in the spring. At this time they begin to hear. In the autumn the ears close, i.e. from autumn until the spring they do not hear. Likewise the shaman's ears begin to hear better in the spring. The kam also have moon ears with which they communicate with the spirits and then re-tell what was conveyed to those present.

3. 'May your judgment-decision come to pass' - The kam arriving at the "deserted churt" finds the grave of the former housewife in order to learn of her thoughts.

4. 'As I walked I had healing substance', - Throughout the whole journey the kam speaks incantations in which he refers to healing substances and magical incantations. This is evidently essential for protection from evil spirits.

5. 'Seven rivers I shall wade across, and then a colt I shall sacrifice' - Along the way the kam figuratively sacrifices a colt.

6. 'What judgment will your lying body pass on us?' - Reaching the grave of the mother the kam disturbs her spirits in order to know of their decision or judgment.

7. 'Whatever payment you demand I make to bless her' - Having disturbed the spirits of those long passed from life the kam makes them offerings.

8. 'You have put it level with the thirty-headed fire mother,
I will put the level of the mourning head of sorrowful flame with holy water' - Having disturbed the mother's grave and learned of her decision the kam tries to quiet her. Then the kam returns the way he came. On the return journey he pronounces words of incantation for a long time. 160. 'May grasped hands fall to the side. May the worried heart be calmed'.

Additional Note: The kam calls his spirit-helpers 'ugalchi' which means 'listener' whereas he calls the woman 'The one with skirt': 'In the hands of the one with skirt, it seems, o-o!'

English Language Translator's Notes to the Shamanic Verse

a. In an article by D.A. Funk analysing material on shamanic drums collected by A. Anokhin he writes: Of particular interest is the anthropomorphic figure 'Shor eezi' on a sledge in which a horse is harnessed. Shor eezi drives the horse with the help of long reins.' Other diagrams of Shor shamanic drums show abundant images of the kam riding a horse holding long reins in one hand.

b. 'Semantically the shaman's rattle can be compared to his lash and whip; in shamanic texts the rattle is described through the symbolism of these objects.' E.N. Romanova

c. It is possible that the image of the rocking shoulders and head is a reference to the peculiar movements that kam make during kamlanie.

d. In the Russian translation 'Kyrchyn' is translated as a thin reed whereas actually 'kyrchyn' is a type of Juniper called in Turkic languages 'Archyn'. This is a sacred tree the branches of which are used in cleansing and smudging rituals.

e. 'May the head of 'kyrchyn' be rounded, may the end of the lash be untied, may the head of the game bones shine,' – these lines are very similar to those found in epic texts where a blessing to the people and land is an essential element of the early text. 'May the head of kyrchyn be rounded' – when kyrchyn is young and growing well the ends of the branches seem soft and round. 'May the end of the lash be untied' – the lash used for driving cattle is usually untied slightly at the end which makes a particular sound as the lash is cracked. 'May the head of the game bones shine' – Turkic people traditionally used bones in games. If the bones are handled they take on a shiny quality. If kyrchyn grows well, if the people have cattle and they play their traditional games then all is well in the land.

f. Securing the supporting pole in the house is symbolic of the restoration of order after chaos, the returning of health to the sick. The axis pole is also symbolic of the world axis, tree or mountain that holds the three worlds in place.

KAMLANIE VERSE TWO: "The Deserted Churt"
Shaman Anis'ya Afanas'evna Tudegesheva

A-ek, waist belt,
A-ek, loosen my right shoulder. 1
A-ek, look kindly, supreme judges
A-ek, watch how they will judge.
(Laughs)
Beyond the village boundary, in the taiga, - he says,
Let's turn around and watch, - he says,
A-ei, tethering post* (setting out, see a. below) on a journey,
loosen both (my) shoulders,
A-ei, my mouth-tongue, leave for the journey.

10. Turn around and look.
A-ek-ai, a-ek, look, look.
A-ek, look supreme judges,
A-ek, which side you will end up on
       (you will spill onto the earth) – he says,
A-ek, watch with understanding (the place)
(you) both will find yourselves.
(Beats the glove).
A-ek, there is the Anzass river,
E-ei, here I am on the bank (of the river)
E-ei, Journeying, I will shift
To those times
A-ei, let's try to return (to those times).

20. E-ei, from my homeland
E-ei, (once) having come (here)
E-ei, girl, dig
A-ei, the founder-seed, of the family-surname.
A-ei, moving to the clan, - he says,
A-ei, in the proper way, digging, shift.
(Beats the glove.)
Ai, digging...

A-ei, yes, there, they calmly gather (together)
A-ei, (All) the seed of the family-surname,
seed of the family-surname, - he says,
A-uk, ai, (All) the seed of the family-surname,
seed of the family-surname, - he says,

30. Which is their day, - he says,
Carefully, little by little, - he says,
Will it return (to us) for a moment? - he says,
A-ii, look, look, - he says,
E-ei, ekh, (Here are) the shoulders-arms of the court of your
     family-surname.
Ai, look, look, - he says,
A-ei, (Here is) the flesh (breast) of the day,
The Che ezi has returned their day (to us), it seems,
A-ei, They are present, mounted with harness,
A-ei, (Here is) the girl who was born, - he says,

40. Ai, She is blessed, - he says,
A-ei, when the flesh (body) of their day opens,
A-ei, the day will not disappear (die),
     Is that not right?, - he says,
A-ei, Which is their day?, - he says,
Ai-ei, shining, it has spilt through (to the earth) – he says,
A-ei, they have risen, with harness.
A-ei, look, look, the day is closed (inaccessible),
A-ei, look, for it is closed, - he says.
A-ei, when its wide leaves blossomed, - he says,
A-ei, when my water (sprinkled as an offering) spilt, - he says,

50. A-ei, then (that) day was closed, - he says.
Ai-ei, from which direction, from which direction
A-ei, to enter (it)?
A-ei, holding on tightly (until it hurts),
A-ei, those who are inside the day, - he says,
A-ai, those who are inside the day, - he says,

Inside the day they are, they are inside the day, - he says,
A-ei, those who are inside the day,
A-ei, let her in (inside).
A-ei, into the body of the day, - he says,

60. A-ei, (there) inside they are, - he says,
Ai, (to) open the doors (to the right),
A-ei, now, if they ask for a portion-head,
A-ei, then, considering (the cost) (she) will stand, - he says,
A-ei, for the body of the day is immense,
A-ei, for the body of the day is unstable,
A-ug (Laughs and beats the glove).
Ai-ek, those who are inside (the day), - he says,
A-ei, those who are outside (the day), - he says,
A-ei, how should it be counted?
A-ei, how should it be understood?

70. From where...yai.
If those who are inside (the day)
see a dark spirit, - he says,
A-ei, being quick and nimble, - he says,
they will put the evil spirit in a sack
Taking the nearest stallion.
A-ei, the blessed one, look,
Look, one with buttons, - he says,
at the saddle with the soft edges
Surely you recognise it? – he says.

80. A-ei, Which direction will she come from?
Ei, When I sprinkled the offering
E-ei, she was reserved,
E-ei, one cannot enter one's home,
the black taiga like that.
E-ei, into the great taiga
E-e, she has flown,
E-ek, descending easily downwards,

E-e, she has flown
E-ei, In the morning at dawn.

90. E-ei, 'ok', look,
At the saddle with the soft edges, he says.
Ai, - she is familiar, - he says,
A-ei, look, listen, - he says,
A-ek, my blessed girl, - he says,
E-ei, How shall I know the truth? - he says,
A-ei, my day, - he says,
A-ei, will pass.
A-ei, on which day,
A-ei entering into the day we will return there.

100. E-ei, my blessed one,
A-ei, the one with guardian-angel,
A-ek, look, look,
One with buttons, - he says,
A-ei, (You) will become quiet,
A-ei, in their impenetrable darkness,
Ik, with corporal day (with flesh and body), - he says,
You let it pass by, - he says,
A-ei, having corporal day, - he says,
She didn't surely pass it by, - he says,

110. The one with skirt, - he says.[2]
A-ei, with which day, - he says,
Entering into the day, she has returned, - he says.
A-ei, Where will she come from?
E-ek, (here is) the path by which she travelled.
E-ei, I do not reproach her.
Ei, the road by which she travelled,
E-ei, I do not reproach her.
E-ek, the day she visited is filled with news,
A-ei, don't turn her back.

120. A-ei, I dress in nine coats of mail, 3
A-ei, I dress in seven coats of mail.
E-ei, be girded at the waist,* (b. below) be girded at the waist.
O-ok.

Notes to the Shamanic Verse

No. 2. "Eski Churt"
(Kam Tudegesheva A., sound recording, interpretation and translation from Shor to Russian by L.N. Arbachakova)

1. The Shor text is softened here which is characteristic for Chilissu-Anzasskii speech.

2. 'The one with skirt, he said.' - This is how the kam figuratively refers to the individual who has come to them for healing.

3. 'A-ei, I dress in nine coats of mail,' - At the end of a kamlanie almost all the kam robe their 'patient' in armour, i.e. a protective aura.

English Language Translator's Notes to the Shamanic Verse

a. The tethering post falls into the same semantic group as the tree of life and world mountain being the 'axis' which holds order in the world of potential chaos.

b. Among the Turkic peoples of Siberia 'girding' oneself or another either with a belt or long piece of material wrapped about the waist is generally used as a protection ritual to shield the main chakhra at the navel from dark substances or spirits.

AFTERWORD

Photo: Alexander Arbachakov

Interior of Shor Home

Shor kam to this day remember the traditions associated with conducting shamanic ritual. Where it has become impossible to conduct certain aspects of these rituals such as blood sacrifice, the element is included without actually carrying out the physical sacrifice. In his 'kamlanie' K. Chudekov for example, conducted a purely symbolic stallion sacrifice.

As mentioned above, the texts of shamanic verse performed by contemporary Shor kam are published here in English for the first time. It has been our aim to show that among the Shor people, the tradition of turning to the kam, mediator between the spirit and human worlds, primarily for healing but also for cleansing one's home or searching for lost cattle, is still very much alive.

Unfortunately, until very recently, no researcher has seriously carried out studies into this aspect of the Shor culture.

Shamanism as a social institution represents an alloy that combines a system of views on the model of the universe with the traditional oral transmission of fundamental knowledge, rites and laws. In previous times, almost every Shor 'ulus' - village, had its kam who played a significant role in the life of the villagers.

Together with the kaichi* - the traditional keepers of the culture, the 'tellers' - the kam were the real keepers of the people's knowledge and culture. Time and History would have it, however, that they are now gradually disappearing.

It is essential that we learn and preserve all that the kam know and remember. Without its language, traditions and memory of the ancestors, a nation becomes moribund. Today the Shor people number only 12,000 in total.

Alexander and Luba Arbachakov

* 'Kaichi' - is a person, traditionally a man, who performs guttural throat singing and retells epic works and other oral texts. The 'kaichi' are the keepers of the oral history and culture. The gift of 'kai' is said to come only to those who have been chosen by the spirits of the natural world. Whilst performing 'kai' the 'kaichi' becomes a sort of resonator transforming the energy of the environment around him.

GLOSSARY

Shor words used in the shamanic verses:

адамныг - (adamnyng) Blessed one, earth, God, My father (Erlik – translator's addition)

аламнынг - (adamnyng)one with guardian-angel

ашкыйак - (ashkyiak) barrier, obstacle, fence, wall

аба чыш - (aba chysh) Gornaya Shoraya Taiga

аймак - (aimak) a region of villages

куйак - (kuiak) armour (in shamanism a specific protective aura)

пÿгÿрге - (pugurge) to bend, curve, roll, turn

Тунег - (tuneg) satisfaction; charge

шакпы - (shakpy) scythe

шийерге - (shiierge) write, draw, underline; realize, accomplish, implement, occur, arise, decide

чаргы - (chargy) court, punishment, court matter, suit, action, competition

Чачак - (chachak) arrow, bow

Чиг - (chig) hem, edge, coat-breast, lapel

шог, шогай - (shog, shogai) interjection during kamlanie

тула - (tula) widower

кес, кеес - (kes, kees) to make a journey (of a shaman and his spirit-helper)

тöс - (tos) the shaman's spirit-helper

туйук - (tuiuk) reserved, secretive, veiled

кор - (kor) abundant

чидек - (chidek) rein, reins

кибер - (kiber) custom/ritual, tradition

олат - (olat) place (in the ether)

тенне - (tenne) compare; measure, evaluate, appreciate

пус - (pus) sacrificial steam

REFERENCE LIST

Alekseev N.A. *Shamanism Tyurkoyazychnikh narodov Sibiri.* Novosibirsk: 'Nauka', 1984. 232 / 1991.

Bedurov B.Y. *Slovo ob Altae.* Gorno-Altaisk, 1990. 379

Burnakov V.A. *Dusha v traditsionnikh vozzreniyakh khakacov* // Journal. Gumanitarnie nauki v Sibiri. Novosibirsk: Publishers CO RAN, 2003. 15-19.

Butanaev V.Y. *Traditsionnaya kul'tura i byt Khakasov.* Abakan: *'Khakasskoe knijhnoe izdatel'ctvo'*, 1996. 221

Butanaev V.Y. *Khakassko-russkii ictoriko-etnograficheskii slovar'.* Abakan, 1999. 236.

Chudoyakov A.I. *Devyat' bubnov shamana.* Kemerova, 1989. 141.

Chudoyakov A.I. *Etyudy shorskogo eposa.* Kemerevo, 1995. 221.

Dyrenkova N.P. *Shorskii Fol'klor.* – M.- L., 1940. 448

D'yakonova V.P. *Altaitsi.* – Gorno-Altaisk: 'Gorno-Altaiskoe knijhnoe izdatel'stvo "Uch Syumer", 2001. 221.

Funk D.A. *Teleutskoe shamanstvo.* –M., 1997. 267

Gmelin I.G. *Puteshestvie po Sibiri. Shorskii sbornik.* – Kemerevo, 1994. p. 9-16

Katsyuba D.V. *Dukhovnaya kul'tura teleutov.* Kemerevo, 1989. 141.

Kimeev V.M. *Shortsi. Kto oni?* – Kemerevo, 1989. 187

Khlopina I.D. *Gornaya Shoriya i shorsti* // Journal Etnograficheskoe obozrenie. ?2, 1992, 134-146 (from earlier article).

Potapov L.P. *Altaiskii shamanism* .- L.: Nauka, 1991. 319.

Radlov V.V. *Iz Sibiri. Stranitsi dnevnika.* M., 1989. 198-210 (Translation from the German original 1893.)

Romanova, E.N. Sakha Ethnographer

SHC *Shorskii sbornik.* First Edition. – Kemerova, 1994. 283

Verbitskii V.I. *Altaiskie inorodtsi* M., 1893, (reprinted edition. Gorno-Altaisk, 1993) 268.

ABOUT THE AUTHORS

Alexander Arbachakov was born within the Shortsi Aboriginal group of southern Siberia in 1964 and raised in the traditional indigenous village of Ust – Kabyrsa. Arbachakov is an environmentalist - a forestry specialist who participated as an expert in the ecological examinations of various bills of the Kemerovskaya region. His area of expertise includes special conservation of wildlife territories as well as general ecologies. As vice-president of the Shortsi People's Association, Alexander Arbachakov takes great pride in recording the beauty of his homeland – the natural beauty of the Shor Mountain region and its indigenous people - through the media of photography and film. Alexander's photos have been exhibited in the Kemerovskaya region.

Lubov Arbachakova Ph.D. (Tudegesheva) was born in 1963 in the small village of Onzas, in the heart of the Mountains Shoria. Luba grew up as one of seven children of the Tudegeshevyh family. Remoteness from the city center dictated the family's daily course of existence - conducting housekeeping for four cows, one per brother; three horses, one per sister; as well as horned cattle, hens, geese, ducks, and those animals found in any household in rural Siberia. Luba is an environmentalist as well as a folklorist and philology specialist, graduated from the Novokuznetsk Pedagogical Institute. She is chief field specialist of Shortsi folklore and ethnography. In addition to this work, Luba is known for her creative expression through painting and poetry.

To learn more about the indigenous Shor tribe of Siberia or to support the efforts of the Shortsi People's Association, contact Alexander and Luba Arbachakov at belsu@rikt.ru Donations can be sent to the "Shortsi People's Association" in care of the Arbachakovs at: 9 Zagorodnaya St., Mezhdurechensk, Kemerovskaya region, 652870, RUSSIA.

Moon Books invites you to begin or deepen your encounter with Paganism, in all its rich, creative, flourishing forms.

SOME RECENT O BOOKS

The Way Beyond the Shaman
Birthing a New Earth Consciousness
Barry Cottrell
"The Way Beyond The Shaman" is a call for sanity in a world unhinged, and a template for regaining a sacred regard for our only home. This is a superb work, an inspired vision by a master artist and wordsmith. **Larry Dossey, MD**, author of *The Extraordinary Healing Power Of Ordinary Things*
9781846941214 208pp £11.99 $24.95

Plant Spirit Wisdom
Sin Eaters and Shamans: The Power of Nature in Celtic Healing for the Soul
Ross Heaven
The Joseph Campbell of our times. **James Shreeve**, *Guardian* journalist
9781846941238 224pp £9.99 $19.95

The Gods Within
An interactive guide to archetypal therapy
Peter Lemesurier
When I saw "The Gods Within", I had to pick up the book. This text includes a personality diagnostic, made up of keywords describing various personality traits. Using this easy to use system, the reader then finds out which Greek God or Goddess archetype that he or she most needs to explore. Ten main personality types are thoroughly described with a number of subcategories slightly modifying each. The reader is then encouraged to explore and embrace this archetype through a series of exercise: self-enquiry, invocation, meditation, and remedial activities. **Dr Tami Brady**, TCM Reviews
1905047991 416pp £14.99 $29.95